WINDMILL ON THE PRAIRIE

Yvonne Hollenbeck

Yvonne Hollenbeck

Poetry about my life on a South Dakota cattle ranch

*Dedicated to all those hardy men and
women who paved the way for us.*

Windmill on the Prairie

Poetry about my life on a South Dakota Cattle Ranch
© 2022 Yvonne Hollenbeck

Contact:
Yvonne Hollenbeck
30549 291st Street
Clearfield, SD 57580
www.yvonnehollenbeck.com
geetwo@gwtc.net
(605) 557-3559

All rights reserved. No part of this book may be reproduced
or transmitted in any form or by any means without written
permission from the author, except brief quotations for purposes
of review.

Cover photography:
Chris Gentry, Sandhills Cattle Rancher of Whitman, Nebraska

Printed by Publication Printing of Nebraska, Inc.

ISBN: 979-8-218-09582-6
Library of Congress Control Number

WINDMILL ON THE PRAIRIE

If I could paint a picture of the finest place on earth,
it would never be of buildings, pay no matter what they're worth.
There'd be no canvas covered with a village, neat and quaint;
a windmill on the prairie is what I'd choose to paint.

Now, you may think it silly that anyone could see
beauty in a windmill, but they mean a lot to me.
Like a lighthouse to a sailor, they're a symbol of the West,
of life that's free and easy and a lifestyle that's the best.

To me there's nothing better than to be out there with God,
smelling clover-scented grasses or fresh raindrops on the sod.
To hear the rustling of the trees, the lowing of the herds,
or watch a hawk that's circling low, then chased away by birds.

Gold itself cannot compare with what a windmill is worth,
bringing forth the fresh cold water from deep beneath the earth,
and when evening shadows lengthen, like a tower in the night
a windmill on the prairie is such a pretty sight.

You can have the Eiffel Tower or the Vatican in Rome,
sky-scrapers in the cities or the fanciest of homes.
The simple, upright beauty that will put them all to test
is a windmill on the prairie when the sun sets in the West.

CONTENTS

Windmill On The Prairie vii

INDEX OF TITLES

Affair (The) 1
A Good Name 2
A Horse Nobody'd Want 3-4
Banker and Insurance Man (The) 5-6
Beef and Beans 7
Benefit (The) 8
Big "Oh No!" (The) 9
Branding Time 10
Calving Time 11-12
Class Reunion (The) 13-14
Committeeman (The) 15-16
Country School (The) 17-18
Cowboy and the Quilter 19-20
Cowboy Fashion Show 21-22
Cowman's Calculations 23-24
Daylight Saving Time 25
Dining Out 26
Father's Boots 27
Feed Salesmen Don't Lie 28
Flag Out on the Ranch 29
Fly a Flag For Josiah 30-31
Frieda's Purse 32
Give Your Horse Its Head 33-35
Good Cow (The) 36
Gourmet Code of the West (The) 37-38
Helpmate (The) 39
Home Town Shopping 40-41
Junk Food Bachelor 42
Kid Broke Pony 43
King of the Internet Cowboys 44

ix

Lucky Farmer	45
March Winds	46
Meal Time	47
Money in Horses	48
My Driver	49
Nature's Church	50
Nothing to Do	51
Oakie and the Skunk	52-54
Old Cowboy (The)	55-56
Old Eagle Eye	57
Old Folks Rodeo	58-60
Old Nellie	61
Pedigree (The)	62
Perfect Grandparents	63-64
Pity the Fool	65-66
Pulling the Caking Truck Blues	67-68
Putting Down Old Red	69-71
Ranch Rig (The)	72-73
Ranch Wife's Top Ten List	74-75
Rancher Wannabe	76
Rebel Rouser	77-78
Roper's Wife's Lament	79
Sorting Time	80-81
Sure a Lot of Work	82
Truth About Cowboy Laundry (The)	83-84
Truth in Advertising	85-86
Watch What You Pray For	87
What I Really Need's a Wife	88
What Would Martha Do?	89-90
While-Yer-At-It	91
Whose Idea?	92-93
Woman's Worst Fear	94-95

POEMS FOR HOLIDAYS and SPECIAL OCCASIONS

A Senior New Years Eve 98
All American Christmas 99-100
Best Gift I Had In Years (The) 101-102
Christmas Grammar Lessons 103
Did You Ever Think of Me? 104
Halloween Headlines 105-106
Heinous Husband Award (The) 107-108
Holiday Makeover 109
How The Poor Folks Are
   Doing This Year 110-111
O Come All Ye Faithful 112
Our Fresh Cut Christmas Tree 113-114
Thanksgiving on the Range 115-116
Valentine Memories 117-118

THE AFFAIR

He thought that I was sleeping
when he came sneaking in;
but he didn't fool me one bit,
I knew where he had been.

It happened several times before
but I once heard someone say,
"That if you just ignore it,
then it might go away."

I know he really cares for her,
I've seen it in his eyes,
and her name is often mentioned
when he talks with other guys.

He's spent a lot of cash on her
and I've never said a word.
When he told me she was special,
I said, "I know...I've heard."

I know they used to rodeo,
that was well before my time.
He said she'd helped him win a lot
and that's why he treats her fine.

Last night it finally ended
when he told me where he'd been.
He said that he was sorry
and he won't sneak out again.

That note left on my pillow
really gave me quite a jolt.
It said, "Dear, I'm out with Cricket,
and she's finally had her colt!"

A GOOD NAME

There's a place over East in a valley
   where the buildings are weathered and old;
it once was somebody's homestead
   full of dreams of a future, I'm told.

I wonder each time I go by there
   just how long they have been all alone;
how long that it's been since that house there
   was once some family's home.

The barn is still standing quite stately,
   though the roof has begun caving in;
and I'm sure that it won't be too long now
   before it's downed by a strong prairie wind.

It's so sad to see just the remnants
   of what once was somebody's pride.
Did they leave because of some hard times
   or was it because someone died?

You can see where they planted some lilacs,
   there's a piece of an old iron fence;
a rusty old pump still sits on a well,
   though I doubt it's been used ever since.

I guess it is like many other
   old places that's left to decay,
reminding us time waits for no one,
   and that too soon there will come a day

when our lives will be like that homestead;
   and treasures that we might possess
will weather and long be forgotten,
   no matter how great your success.

Glen Hollenbeck's story about his horse, "Punch," who helped him win the 2002 U.S. Calf Roping Championship, plus many other ropings; then carried a young college girl to numerous championships.

A HORSE NOBODY'D WANT

I bought Punch from a trader who didn't know his age;
and said he'd lost the papers but, *he's ten* by what he'd gauge.
T'was a darned good looking gelding, but looks are just skin-deep;
it's heart and disposition that wins money you can keep.

At first he'd hump and try to buck, but that was not as bad
as when you'd go to bridle him...the worst I ever had.
He'd obviously been beaten on the head and by the ears;
you still can't touch his right one and it's now been several years.

After weeks of gentle treatment, that horse became my friend,
he paid me back ten-fold the way things turned out in the end.
And why someone was mean to him, I often wonder why,
but know there are bad horsemen...a fact we can't deny.

I trained him for a calf horse and a good one he'd become;
he'd track a calf, stop real good, and my, how he could run!
We tried to sell him several times but no one wanted him,
they'd take him home and try him out and bring him back again.

One old dolly thought he'd make a good horse for her son,
but tried him out and changed her mind before the deal was done.
Some windy guy from Texas saw him working rope one day
and offered cold hard cash if he could have a year to pay.

There were several tough young ropers that turned their back on him
and searched for better horses that just might help them win.
Then my buddy, Arlen, told me not to sell that horse
as he might become a winner, and he was right, of course.

Soon the horse nobody'd wanted started turning lots of heads
because together we were winning as the word began to spread
that this was quite a rope horse, then calls began to come
to see if I would sell this horse they'd heard was number one.

I'd say, *this horse is not for sale,* and that just suits me fine
because he and I are having fun a-winning most the time.
And when I want another one that'll put me out in front,
I think I'll just go looking for a horse nobody'd want!

PUNCH and Glen Hollenbeck in action.

THE BANKER AND THE INSURANCE MAN

When the banker pays a visit
to check your inventory
the way he values assets, folks
is quite a different story

than the values placed upon them
by the one who sells insurance;
and if those two would switch their jobs
it would really make a difference.

The first thing that the banker does
is try to claim your land;
he says it's really not worth much
but on the other hand

he needs it for collateral
with the cattle market down;
but he can't loan you cash on it
because it is only ground.

The value of your cattle
is the price the packer pays;
your machinery is not worth a dime
for it's seen its better days.

You can't borrow on a good old horse,
you can't borrow on your wife;
your house ain't worth a tinker's damn
and neither is your life.

BUT HERE COMES YOUR INSURANCE MAN!
He sings a different song;
and says that horse is worth a lot!
You knew that all along.

You really need a policy
just in case it meets its fate;
and you'd better have a BIG one
on your kind and loving mate.

He says she's worth a million
if you figured up the cost
of hiring folks to do her work;
why, she'd really be a loss!

And what about those buildings
that the banker said was junk;
if disaster took just one of them
you really would be sunk!

Why, if lightning hit some cattle,
the loss would be immense;
you have got a hundred thousand
in just windmills, tanks and fence.

When that agent finished tallying
it looked like we were wealthy;
the way he figured assets
made our finances quite healthy.

So I hope you get my point
in them two switching jobs, you see,
because if bankers sold insurance,
not very much you'd need.

But if Insurance Agents
made the agriculture loans,
we'd all be driving brand new cars
and living in new homes.

We'd be looking pretty prosperous,
and live a *"rich man's life."*
Instead of buying life insurance,
you'd just mortgage One Good Wife!

BEEF AND BEANS

It can sometimes be discouraging when you live on a ranch
and try to make a living raising cattle,
With all the regulations and expenses that we face,
this business has become a constant battle.

There are vegetarians claiming, "Beef is bad for you!"
as well as every other form of meat.
Stating lentils, fruits and nuts, and what they call "legumes"
is the only types of food that one should eat.

Then here comes PETA claiming that we torture animals
and never should send any cows to slaughter;
That branding calves is cruel, and so are vaccine guns,
then blame us for why temps are getting hotter.

They say that climate change is coming from our cows
from all the methane gasses they secrete;
and the only remedy, in their scientific minds.
is to get folks to refrain from eating meat.

Now, if livestock is the culprit of global warming as they say,
and their flatulence is truly cause to blame.
If we'd all become a Vegan and refrain from eating meat,
would it stop the climate changes, as they claim?

'Though this might be the answer, if what they state is true;
there still may be a problem, so it seems.
Do they know how much gas that folks will pass
when all they eat is nuts and fruit and beans?

THE BENEFIT

We are fixing to host a benefit
and hope that you folks can all come.
It's for poor ol' Leroy, our neighbor;
he's an unlucky son-of-a-gun.

We will have a pie and soup supper
and there'll be a raffle or two.
The Lutherans are matching the money we get;
Modern Woodman Insurance will too.

In case you've not heard of his troubles,
it happened about six years ago.
He was loading some meat at the Packing Plant
when a push-cart ran over his toe.

He was diagnosed, "Total Disabled!"
He never will work anymore.
He has three little kids, one more on the way,
and the oldest one's just barely four.

And you know with the high cost of living,
disability rarely goes far;
with payments so high on his new pickup truck,
he barely can gas up his car.

His horses need pasture and shoeing;
his practice steers, grain and good hay.
With luck we can raise him some money.
The benefit's next Saturday.

Just in case you don't know him, I'll tell you
he's a good guy; never does dope.
He's a clean-living, talented fellow,
and Leroy can sure enough rope!

THE BIG "OH NO!"

There are sins in this old world of ours
    that would make the devil curse.
Each time you think you've heard it all,
    well, here comes something worse.

But there's one thing that a rancher's wife
    must never, never do;
it's the absolute worst thing of all
    and could be the ruin of you.

I must admit I've come real close
    to crossing that fine line,
but it happened one spring day last year
    to a real good friend of mine.

You could hear her husband holler
    from a couple miles away;
and when I heard just what she'd done
    all I could do was pray

that somehow she'd find forgiveness;
    for that poor old gal had took
a dirty shirt and washed it
    and it contained his Calving Book!

BRANDING TIME

It happens mostly in the spring, when all the calves are here;
excitement builds as plans are made for branding time each year.

The rancher calls a list of names he's jotted in his book,
the wife starts making plans for all the things she has to cook.

He lines up all the vaccine, she bakes a dozen pies,
the day before they set up pens, she feeds a dozen guys.

Then finally branding day arrives, he's lined up quite a bunch
she's lined up dinner, supper, and in between, the lunch.

The more help that the rancher has, the more she has to do.
It takes a lot of beef and beans to feed a branding crew.

(Did I mention that one feller who brought along a brat?
He said his wife could use a break; she wished she'd thought of that!)

After hauling chairs and tables and cooking several days,
the big day's finally over as she goes to bed and prays:

> *If I should die before I wake*
> *I hope I never have to bake*
> *another cake, another pie*
> *in that big ranch up in the sky.*

But soon the rooster's crowing as another day begins
They'll be making plans for next year when it's branding time again.

CALVING TIME

Whether it be spring or fall,
    there is a sure-fire thing;
it's the worst kind of weather
    when the cows begin to spring.

You dare not get too far from home;
    you dare not miss a chance
to be there to assist the cows
    when they're calving on the ranch.

The mud room's clean and orderly,
    supplies are in their place.
When suddenly it happens
    ...a new calf has shown its face!

It's Calving Time!

Two weeks pass by and all is fine,
    we've only lost a few,
but when that blizzard hit last week
    there's not much we could do.

The mud room needs a scrubbing,
    nipple bottles fill the sink;
and after all the calves brought in,
    this place begins to stink.

Another week has passed us by,
    I've nothing to report
except that sleep and patience
    are both getting mighty short.

It's Calving Time!

You can't get in the mud room,
    this place is one big mess.
Why anyone would live this way
    is anybody's guess.

And now just like those calving cows,
    we both are slowing down.
I'm going to watch the springers
    because hubby went to town.

He went in to a bull sale,
    it is like an endless chain.
We'll breed those cows for next year
    and we'll do it all again.

When it's Calving Time!

THE CLASS REUNION

Last year I got invited to the reunion of my class.
It's been years since graduation; my, don't the time go fast?
They said we'd have a real big time, to bring our spouses too;
we'd all get reacquainted and find out what they do.

I hadn't seen those folks in years so felt that I should go,
but my spouse declined. He could not miss the White River Rodeo.
He said that's where he'd meet old friends and I fully understood;
for him to meet those city guys would not be very good.

You see, he's just an old cow hand; he was born here on this ranch,
with no formal education and he would not have much chance
of fitting in their social whirl; and he would not understand
their talk of stocks and Wall Street because he's just an old ranch hand.

I am sure his clothes would not fit in, his faded hate and boots;
because those city guys wear "Ralph Lauren" and costly tailored suits.
But enough about my husband, we went our separate ways;
He loaded up his rope horse and went to White River's Frontier Days.

I went back home to see those folks I had not seen in a long, long time.
First we were to have a social hour; then together, we would dine.
So I bought myself a brand new dress and curled up my hair.
Soon I was in the parking lot, then headed right in there.

At first I thought I'd made an error and got in the wrong place.
I didn't see a soul I knew...not one familiar face.
The men were mostly fat and bald, the women, old and gray.
I thought perhaps I best just leave, when I heard a lady say:

*Come over here and register and wear this little tag
so folks will know just who you are.* Then she began to brag.
She asked, *Don't you remember me? I'm the class homecoming queen.*
Now folks, this gal had changed a lot and I don't want to sound mean.

She'd put on a couple hundred pounds; lost her school-girl frame.
Do you suppose I'm the only one who never really changed?
Then she wanted me to meet her man she'd met some time ago;
she said, *He's just the greatest!* She thought I'd like to know.

She said she met this feller line dancing in some pub;
then said, *The place to meet great guys is by joining a good dance club.*
Then she wanted me to meet him, so she hollered at this guy,
I just stood there flabbergasted and I'll tell you the reason why.

He wore a high-crowned cowboy hat with a big, thick feather band;
with pins stuck on the crown, matching rings on his white, pudgy hands.
He wore about the wildest shirt I think I've ever seen,
and he had his name embroidered on his polyester jeans!

His jeans were neatly tucked inside high-topped, high-heeled boots;
He looked just like Chris Christie wearing a Roy Rogers suit.
There was something shining brightly beneath his belly-fat;
it was a great big, shiny buckle, that resembled a new hub cap!

But the thing that really got me as I chatted with this pair,
was when she told me what he did, as if I really cared.
She said, *My man's a cowboy! I guess it really shows!*
Then asked me what my husband does; I just answered, *I don't know.*

But I know now what a cowboy is, and as I look out there
I see a bunch of imposters, you fellers in those chairs.
You dress just like my husband; I know some of you are ranchers too;
but I know that you aren't Cowboys; you don't dress the way they do!

While watching a rodeo at Gordon, Nebraska, I could not help but notice the late Dick Louks, a committeeman, working the chute gate, picking up flanks, etc., while riders basically ignored him as if he were in the way. Little did they realize that in his day he could outride any one of them. He and his brother, Wayne Louks, were saddle bronc legends in the early days of professional rodeos.

THE COMMITTEEMAN

He opens the chute, as the bronc rider nods
and he's sure to get out of the way;
He watches the ride as the old sorrely bucks
as he thinks 'bout a long-ago day.

It wasn't that long ago, though it seems,
when it was him crawling onto the best.
He'd measure his hack, pull down his hat.
and his rides stood apart from the rest.

Just the sound of his name brought crowds to their feet
as an old hand pulled open the gate.
He'd ride like they'd never seen broncs rode before,
but Old Father Time was his fate.

Now, there's few in the stands that remember his name
and to all these young hands, he's unknown;
but little they know as they ride in their prime
that too soon it will be them, all alone.

He picks up a flank, tosses it back to the chute,
as his mind wanders back to that day
when it was him on a bronc with his hack held up tight
nodding to an old man on the gate.

My cousin, Boyd Anderson of Fir Mountain, Sask, another good bronc rider from the era of the Louks boys. Like so many, WWII interfered with their rodeo career. In fact, Boyd spent considerable time in a German Prisoner of War Camp.

THE COUNTRY SCHOOL

They closed our Country School last year;
    it was sad to see it go.
But they claim it's for the better,
    and to some, that may be so.

They say that modern children
    need a better education,
And those one-room country schools
    are not a real good situation.

Now, I wonder how so many folks
    ever got to be so smart
when a one-room country schoolhouse
    was where they got their start.

Then I think about my little girls
    with their lunch pails in their hands,
a-headin' off to country school
    and to them it was just grand!

They didn't ride a school bus,
    just a good old saddle horse;
with no special hot lunch programs,
    just a boxed lunch was the course.

There was no big gymnasium
    but those kids sure learned to run
a-playing tag and other games
    ...their recess was such fun.

They didn't have computers
    but they learned to read and write
and figure change and multiply
    ...they learned it all in spite

of lacking all the modern things
    that they will get in town;
I suppose that's why the country schools
    are one by one closed down.

The School Boards call it "progress,"
    as for me, I call it "fate."
When we climb another step in life,
    we close another gate.

A one room country school house
    these days are seldom seen;
and with their passing also goes
    a time much more serene.

Although they closed the school down
    it will never quite depart,
because its special memories
    will live within my heart.

Churchside School near Clearfield, SD

COWBOY and the QUILTER

Did she know the consequences
   when she became his wife?
Or was she just enthralled
   with exciting cowboy life.

She had seen a lot of movies
   with Roy and Dale and Gene;
and to be a cowboy's sweetheart
   was beyond her wildest dreams.

So, when she met her cowboy
   with his horses and his ranch,
she knew at once she was in love
   and quick to take the chance.

But what those movies don't portray
   and what she did not know
was all the chores she'd have to do
   in sun and rain and snow.

The men she'd have to cook for;
   the dirty laundry piles;
the orphan calves she'd have to feed;
   no neighbor gals for miles.

They claim she went to pieces
   when she moved on his range.
Now, I won't say she's crazy,
   but she is a little strange.

After all she buys new fabric,
   then cuts it all apart,
then sews it back together,
   which proves she's not too smart.

But the boys in the bunkhouse
   have nice quilts on all their beds;
and in lieu of woolen saddle pads,
   there's patchwork ones instead.

They make a happy couple
   and he doesn't seem to mind
that the sink is full of dishes
   and the housework's all behind.

Although the ranch is quite neglected,
   neither harbors guilt;
as he rides the range on his ol' horse
   she just sits and pieces quilts.

*Painting by cowboy artist, Dave Price;
Valentine, Nebraska*

COWBOY FASHION SHOW

As cowboys head toward my kitchen
after branding calves today,
my front porch takes resemblance
of a fashion-show runway.

First comes a short young cowboy,
I think his name is "Lance",
he's in a blue BUM tee-shirt
and some denim wrangler pants.

He wears a pair of tennis shoes,
 a weathered baseball cap;
"Thank-you Lance!" And here we have
another well-dressed chap.

Charles wears a striped shirt
stretching over his spare tire;
a pair of lace-up ropers
is his choice of foot attire.

Again, a pair of Wranglers
are the pants he chose to wear;
but he'd look a darned sight better
if he wore a bigger pair.

Here comes handsome Richard
in a shirt that's starched and clean;
his nice physique accentuates
the way he wears his jeans.

His choice of boots are Justins;
he puts them all to test
in his silver belly Stetson hat
and rugged leather vest.

The last old cowboy hobbles up
and he is quite a sight;
he looks just like a street bum
that has just been in a fight.

His poor old hat is filthy
and is badly out of shape;
his boots would be in pieces
if it wasn't for *Duct Tape*.

His Wranglers are all bloodstained;
he must have been the one
that did the castrating,
 . . . the job that is no fun.

His poor old shirt has had it;
the pocket's plum detached,
and has two buttons missing.
His wife must never patch!

Then I recognize the buckle,
"Champion Roper '84"
Why, it's Glen, my poor old husband
 that comes walking thru the door!

COWMAN'S CALCULATIONS

It's a long way to the Orient,
    or from here to Calgary,
and many miles to places
    like the Mediterranean Sea.
But perhaps the greatest distance
    that one can calculate
is the space between a newborn calf
    and the steak that's on your plate.

There's a lot of cash invested
    long before that calf is born
in bulls and cows and pastureland,
    in vaccine, hay and corn.
Not every calf survives its birth,
    not every cow will live,
no matter how much tender care
    the cattleman can give.

Several months of constant care
    and miles in saddle leather;
the rancher never takes a break
    no matter what the weather.
And no one's ever guaranteed
    his pastures will withstand
drought and other troubles
    dealt from Mother Nature's hand.

In the meantime he spends thousands
    on supplies to put up hay
and hopes he has enough to get him
    through each winter day.
Most everything he needs to buy
    continues to get higher
like diesel fuel, tractor parts,
    tires, posts and wire.

Then calves are weaned and some will die
    just going through the stress;
how many will survive through this
    is anybody's guess.
Then, after all the trials
    that a cowman must go through,
here comes folks from PETA
    saying, *beef's not good for you.*

But we know that beef is healthy
    for those folks are all dead wrong
and the cowman will continue
    what he's been doing all along;
'though most have mangled fingers
    from a squeeze-chute accident,
or one or two that's missing
    and a back that's weak and bent.

So, "hats off" to the cowman
    for the troubles he goes through
providing safe and tasty beef
    for folks like me and you.
And remember all the miles,
    and the many steps it takes
to take you from a newborn calf
    to the steak that's on your plate.

DAYLIGHT SAVING TIME

I missed a meeting yesterday because I was home in bed;
it seems that I had darned sure failed to set my clock ahead.
Daylight Saving Time can sure play havoc on my mind,
because when I need to spring ahead, I usually fall behind.

Our poor old cows don't care about the time or in what zone.
I wish they'd make us all the same and leave our clocks alone.
It is really hard to figure out the art of saving time.
Do you put it in a piggy bank like a penny or a dime,

Or stick it in a fruit jar, or stuff it in a sock?
I'd rather we'd just leave it be and keep it in the clock.
And what about the daylight that this time change will create?
Will it help relax our schedules when we are running late?

I wonder just who thought this up; by now he's probably dead;
I hope his hour of passing was behind and not ahead.
But if he's still alive I hope they charge him with a crime
for messing with our lives creating Daylight Saving Time.

DINING OUT

When you live out in the country, it's really quite a treat
when maybe once or twice a year you might go out to eat.

It happened once last summer after helping put up hay,
my husband asked if I would like to eat in town that day.

Well, I was quick to answer "Yes!" Then hurried to prepare;
I changed into my best old dress and fixed my windblown hair.

In nothing flat, our pickup truck was headed down the lane;
a dinner date with hubby was like lighting an old flame!

I'm visualizing candlelight as music softly plays.
imagining the kindly things to me he just might say!

And as the pickup bounced along, I thought of even more;
when at the edge of town we pulled up to the old feed store.

I told him I would wait outside while he picked up some feed
for the guy that usually waits on him don't have a lot of speed.

Besides my shoes were killing me, I thought I'd rest my feet.
He said: "You'd better come on in if you would like to eat."

Then pointed to a banner on the door that I could read
for the annual pancake supper at the local Feed and Seed!

SEQUEL:

With headlights pointing out, we headed to the ranch,
and we both laughed and talked about our "evening of romance."

But next week is his birthday so instead of grilling steaks,
I'll just invite his buddies out and fix them all pancakes.

FATHER'S BOOTS

I like to wear my father's boots
and act just like him too;
because he is just the nicest guy
a feller ever knew.

He lets me go outside with him
and help him do the chores;
he's showed me how to swing a loop
and ride my little horse.

I hope when I am all grown up
his boots will fit me then;
because if I am a father too,
I'd like to be like him!

Glen Hollenbeck, age 3, in his father's boots.

FEED SALESMEN DON'T LIE

We were sure struggling a-raising our cattle;
it seemed that a profit was not to be found.
Our debt was a-growing and we were sure worried
until a feed salesman stopped by on his round.

He showed us a product that he was now selling
that was guaran-darn-teed to add fifty pounds;
only a fool would fail to not buy it.
We knew at that moment salvation was found.

It's normal to wean off a five hundred pounder;
a few good bull calves might weigh a tad more.
But buying that feed would sure be the ticket
for adding more pounds, then our profits would soar.

That got us to thinking about all of the products
that promise to increase your profits and gain.
We bought us some Smartlic, some fly tags and Warbex,
and soy-based high protein energized grain.

Pfizer invented some weight-gain injections,
we bought Ivomec to rid parasites;
Lick tubs were added to our cattle rations
with special injections to whet appetites.

Then a computer with cattle gain programs
was something we thought would be handy to have.
We were astonished when checking the outcome
that we could be weaning some thousand pound calves!

We bought a new pickup, a trailer, a tractor,
with no money down 'till we sell in the fall.
The profits we get from the use of these products
should pay off our debt plus cover this all.

So if you are planning to make it in ranching
you'd best follow suit or your business will die,
and if you would like, I'll send by that salesman
because we are aware that feed salesmen don't lie!

THE FLAG OUT ON THE RANCH

It was an old and faded flag but it was always there,
for everyone to see it freely waving in the air.
He'd say *"I always fly it every time I get a chance,
although I know it's odd to see it out here on this ranch."*

Each morning he would put it up, at night he'd take it down;
it seemed so strange to do this when he lived so far from town.
But when you'd ask about it, his face would beam with joy
he'd tell how he went off to war when he was but a boy.

He said it changed him to a man and changed him much too fast
from scenes imprinted on his mind, but that is in the past.
He lost a lot of buddies but somehow his life was spared;
it pleased him so when folks would fly their flag to show they cared.

Then said, *"I hope you'll fly one, and never take it down
even though you're in the country and a long long way from town.
'cause there's still a lot of people fighting hard to keep us free
although it may be for a cause in which you disagree."*

Now, ever since that day when he explained this all to me
I know just why he flies it when it's just for him to see.
It's to show appreciation for those who gave their best,
and that flag is always flying on his ranch there in the West.

FLY A FLAG FOR JOSIAH

There's a long, lonely road across Nebraska,
where I was driving one hot summer day.
It was there in the Sandhills I saw it,
a flag on a big bale of hay.

It looked rather strange on that meadow,
but soon I was seeing some more.
There were flags on weathered old gate posts.
I wondered what they were there for.

I came to a village called "Wood Lake"
and stopped at a little café;
I needed a break, but casually asked:
"Why are those flags flying today?"

The waitress then told me the reason,
with tears in her eyes, paused to say,
"We're flying those flags for Josiah
because they're bringing him back home today.

He was raised right here in the Sandhills,
but he answered the Nation's call,
and became the finest of soldiers;
to prove it, he gave us his all.

So we're flying those flags for Josiah;
after all, it is all we can do
to show our respect for his service
defending our Red, White and Blue."

I thought of the words that she told me
as I soon headed back on my way,
how it sure wouldn't hurt us to fly them
to show that we care every day.

Because there's more that have fought for our freedom,
and that banner that waves in the sky
is for all of the veterans who fought for that flag
so liberty shall never die.

Those folks gave their all for Old Glory.
Like this lad, we all owe a debt;
By flying a flag in their honor
We're showing we will not forget.

So, let's all fly a flag for Josiah,
and for all other veterans too;
they've all paid a price for our freedom.
After all, it's the least we can do

for those who have sacrificed for us,
It lets them know how much we care;
A symbol how we love our freedom
is that flag flying free in the air.

*In Memory of Spec. Josiah Hollopeter,
killed in Iraq on June 14, 2007*

FRIEDA'S PURSE

Some folks go to museums or browse in antique stores,
others watch shows like "Hoarders" or even "Storage Wars."
But, until your life is over and you're riding in a hearse,
you will never find collections like you'll find in Frieda's Purse.

There's a makeup bag and sewing kit; at least a dozen pens;
note pads found in motels, and empty breath mint tins.
There's at least a hundred Kleenex but most of them are used;
candy, nuts and cookies, a banana badly bruised.

There's a big fat photo album, she likes to show you that
full of pictures of her grandkids and all her dogs and cats.
You'll find a couple western novels, a magazine or two,
and why a dictionary? I haven't got a clue.

A camera and a flashlight, but neither of them works,
and somewhere near the bottom of Frieda's bulging purse
is her billfold and important stuff and often hard to find.
Sometimes hunting for it has put her in a bind

Like the time she got caught speeding; the cop began to curse
as she was looking for her license which was somewhere in that purse.
They say he finally gave up; it was her lucky day
because he just wrote out a warning, gladly heading on his way.

One day her back was hurting so she saw a chiropractor
whose advice was that her pocketbook was probably the factor.
It rather ticked her off when he said it would get worse
if she didn't get a fanny pack and ditch that heavy purse.

I could go on forever listing items in that mess,
but then, to be real honest, I really should confess
that my purse is just about as bad, but one thing I'll concede,
"You never know when in the purse is something you might need."

GIVE YOUR HORSE ITS HEAD

He would saddle up his pony,
    then bundle up real good;
load his gear and check his cinch,
    like every cowboy should.
Then he'd climb up in the saddle,
    feeling happy as a rule,
then down the trail you'd see him lope
    a-headed off to school.

His mom would gladly drive him,
    but he did not want that.
He liked to ride his pony,
    wearing boots and cowboy hat.
He loved the birds and animals
    he'd watch for on the way;
besides, it did his pony good
    to ride him every day.

But one day, during recess time
    the sky got dark and gray;
a call came that a real bad storm
    was headed out that way.
The teacher let the children out,
    the cowboy headed home;
but soon the snow was blinding him;
    he was out there all alone.

He had soon lost his direction
    and thought he'd got off course,
and knew the only chance he had
    was to trust his little horse.
His mom and dad were worried sick;
    all they could do was pray.
Where could their little cowboy be
    as the blizzard raged that day?

They hoped he'd found a neighbor's home
    where he'd be safe and sound;
perhaps he'd stopped at Father Doyle's
    but phone lines were all down.
It seemed like an eternity
    when suddenly they heard
what sounded like a horse outside
    and neither said a word.

They opened up the back porch door
    and shed some tears of joy
when they saw that dear old pony
    and their precious little boy.
Now many years have come and gone,
    the little cowboy's growing old,
remembering still that frightful day,
    the wind, the snow, and cold.

And as we go through life it seems
    there's things that blind our way;
and why we take a dead-end road
    is sometimes hard to say.
But we are all aware that life
    is full of things to dread;
instead of pulling on the reins,
    just give your horse his head.

Glen Hollenbeck and his good pony, Dave, the horse that took him safely home to and from school.

THE GOOD COW

That cow has been a problem
since the day he brought her home.
She won't stay in her pasture
and is always on the roam.

She's torn out several fences
and busted down a gate;
he tried to save the gate post
but he got there way too late.

He tried to pull her calf one time
when it looked like it was stuck,
but she tried to run him down
and caved the side in on his truck.

Another time she took him
when he tried to tag her calf,
and we have to buy a new door
on that angry cow's behalf.

When I told him we should sell her,
I almost had to laugh,
when he said, "We cannot do that,
she'll raise too good a calf!"

THE GOURMET CODE OF THE WEST

It's been a well-known fact for years
    that country cooking's the best.
You are always welcome at dinnertime,
    that's the "Gourmet Code of the West."

Whether you're there shoeing a horse,
    or fixing a tractor that's down;
you're always welcome to eat with the folks,
    there's no sense in going to town.

She'll just throw on another potato,
    the ranch cook knows how to make do
whether she's cooking for ten hungry men
    or just her and her hubby, just two.

I'll bet that you think she's a sweetie,
    a lady that never gets down;
but she loses her pride when she glances outside
    and there's that darned salesman from town!

He shows up each time just at high noon;
    by "each time" I mean once a week;
he's figured it out, on purpose no doubt,
    he just shows up for something to eat.

He eats and he blows about all that he knows,
    then he tries to sell hubby some feed.
She gets up from her chair leaving them sitting there
    because she's thinking just what this dude needs.

She remembers a salad still cold in the fridge,
    the one that last meal no one ate;
the salad she got and in it she tossed
    a cure so he won't constipate.

He ate all those greens, was a terrible thing
    when that laxative started to work.
He left in a hurry, there's no time to worry
    about us buying feed from that jerk.

Well, the story is true of a ranch lady who
    put a greedy feed man to the test;
one who's accused of having abused
    that old "Gourmet Code of the West!"

*1904 at the Spade Ranch, South of Gordon, Nebraska.
The ranch ran 35,000 head of cattle, owned
by founders, Richards & Comstock.
The cook was Jack McCormack.*

Several years ago, just before calving season and spring work was to commence, our hired man quit, so my husband and I did all the work without hired help. One of my husband's friends consistently asked him, "How are you doing all that without a hired man?" My husband would reply, "Yvonne is helping me." Then the friend would say, "Yes, but how are you doing all that without help." It disgusted both of us, so I felt compelled to turn my frustration into a poem.

THE HELPMATE

You say I looked disgusted,
   but you took me by surprise
I suppose there was resentment
   that was coming from my eyes.

Ever since that hired man left
   I've been more than just his wife
I'm the helper by his side
   as he continues ranching life.

I get the gates and scoop the bunks
   and help with feeding hay
and that is just the start of all
   the jobs I do each day.

I'm right there for the calving
   and I help with all the chores
then try to catch my work up
   when I get some time indoors.

You see, I run and jump
   each time he gives a little yelp
and it galls me that you ask
   how he is doing "with no help."

HOME TOWN SHOPPING

I guess I'm just old fashioned
    and I just don't have a clue
about the modern ways of shopping
    that folks nowadays like to do.
But it bothers me that little towns
    are dying, one by one,
and surmise that modern shopping
    is the reason they're undone.

You used to find most anything
    in little one-horse towns,
now most the stores are empty
    with the buildings falling down.
That causes me to wonder,
    "What caused these towns to die?"
Those little towns had everything
    you'd ever want to buy.

Folks never heard of cyberspace,
    they shopped the Five & Dime,
or hardware store, or candy shop,
    where clerks would take the time
to thank you for your business,
    and it sure was safe to say,
the goods you bought were made here
    in the good old USA.

Do you know who you are buying from
    when you shop Cyberspace?
When your little league needs sponsors,
    can you call upon their place?
Are they doing us a favor
    or just taking us for fools,
because they sure don't pay no taxes
    to support our local schools.

I think we should get together
    to form a Shopping Drive
where we buy things from local stores
    and keep these burgs alive.
If you are wanting something special
    and you're really in a bind,
You might shop your hometown stores
    you'd be surprised at what you find.

It might be quite relaxing,
    you would not have far to go
and this shopping drive might play a part
    to help these towns to grow.
I don't need a "Cyber Monday"
    or "Black Friday" shopping spree
because the "Home Town" type of shopping
    is the perfect kind for me.

JUNK FOOD BACHELOR

Batching must be pretty tough
if he would just confess.
It seems whenever I am gone
I come home to a mess.

Oh, the kitchen stove is tidy
because he can't cook or bake;
instead he lives on candy bars
and "Little Debbie Cakes."

I found a lengthy cash receipt
that was from a grocery store.
He'd gone in for a loaf of bread,
but bought a few things more.

Like "Oreos" and donuts,
chips and cheesy snacks;
pretzel rods and "Tootsie Rolls,"
(I counted several sacks).

He'd shot a fifty-dollar bill
for just one loaf of bread;
forgot I'd left good casseroles,
so ate that junk instead.

There was not one ounce of meat
that I noticed on the list,
and I don't want to sound
like some nagging pessimist;

But he put an "Eat Beef" sticker
on the bumper of my car.
I think I'll put one on his pickup
that reads, "Eat A Candy Bar!"

KID BROKE PONY

I found a perfect pony for my grandkid yesterday,
    it was posted by a trader on the net;
There's a lot of horses posted, but this one caught my eye
    and seemed to be the best one I've found yet.
I know you shouldn't buy one from a trader, sight unseen,
    but the guy claimed he was honest as can be;
and after he described the horse, I wired him the cash.
    It sure should fit my grandkid to a tee!

The trader said he got the horse in Utah just last week;
    a little place called Milford, I recall.
The horse don't have no papers, but he's twenty, so he thought
    but you really don't need papers after all.
He had bought him from a rancher who had raised a lot of kids
    but they are all grown up and gone, of course.
But his kids are winning buckles from the training that they got
    just from practicing their riding on that horse.

I only paid ten thousand for this special little steed;
    my grandkid's going to name him "Cracker Jack".
The trader claimed the horse would ride just like a rocking chair
    from having years of kids upon its back,
I just can't wait to get the horse and bring him to my place
    with little Johnny standing by my side.
It sure should be exciting when he crawls upon that horse
    it's the "Wright" kind to help him learn to ride!

SEQUEL:

It's the "Wright" kind of pony for a kid to learn to ride,
    it's the "Wright" kind of horse, make no mistake;
If you don't believe the trader, you might ask the kids
    themselves; just check with maybe Cody, Jess or Jake!
    …or Ryder…Rusty…Stetson
    …Spencer…Alex….Calvin…Statler,
how many kids does that make?

KING of the INTERNET COWBOYS

He's king of the internet cowboys;
he rides for the old FB brand.
He knows everything that a cowman should know,
and a self-proclaimed "heck-of-a-hand."

His crown is a fairly new black Stetson hat;
his throne is a soft, easy chair
There's a "Bronc for Breakfast" print on his wall
and he pretends that he too is right there.

He rises each day at the breaking of dawn,
heads for his range, puts the coffee pot on;
then goes down the hall to take care of his chores;
he's thankful he don't have to do them outdoors.

Then fills up his mug and spends most the day
spreading the bull as he's posting away,
In fact he is known to occasionally boast
that no rancher alive has planted more posts.

In case you are wondering where he got all his knowledge,
it's from a farm and ranch manual he once saw in college.
Then he watched lots of Westerns and studied John Wayne
and all that he learned has imprinted his brain.

I'm sure all you boys who have ranched all your life
are probably amazed at his expert advice.
So, let's give him credit where credit is due;
he's the King of the Internet Cowboy Crew!

LUCKY FARMER

The coon killed all his chickens,
his tractor's engine died;
he couldn't raise a decent crop
no matter how he tried.

His wife had up and left him,
his mortgage was called in;
the bred cows turned up empty,
he just couldn't seem to win.

The world was on his shoulders;
and he had reason to complain,
but he smiled and said, "I'm lucky
because we finally got some rain!"

It's always exciting to have a good singer put my words into a song. That is what happened with this poem, which I co-wrote with the great Texas singer, Jean Prescott.

MARCH WINDS

There's laundry to do and breakfast to get,
these kids have a big appetite.
If the wind don't tear the sheets off the line
we'll sleep in fresh linens tonight.

We're calving heifers and working all hours,
from daylight to dark of the night;
and the wind beats a chill down into my bones
but those babes are a beautiful sight. (Chorus)

Wind caught the screen door and broke it clean off;
shingles blew off of the shed.
Sometimes I walk backwards to get where I'm going;
no wonder I can't get ahead!

I don't even think about wearing a dress,
except to our church on the Lord's Day.
I'm holding my skirt down while loading up kids
while my Sunday School notes blow away. (Chorus)

Sometimes I think it will blow me away,
don't know just when it will end.
The weatherman says it will die down tonight,
but tomorrow will come up again.

Soon will come summer and all of the heat
and we'll be checking cattle one day;
if that windmill's not turning, I'll be a-yearning
for the wind to come blow me away.

CHORUS:
Wind is as wild as a filly in springtime,
blows like a prairie typhoon.
The windmill keeps time like a toe-tapping fiddler
and the tumbleweeds dance to the tune.

MEAL TIME

In this world of mass confusion
and many changes in the land,
terms that are used at meal time
can be hard to understand

Because out here in the country
what we call the food that's served
is not the same way it's described
by a city person's words.

In the morning we serve breakfast
but in town, they call it brunch,
our noon meal is called dinner;
in the city, it's called lunch.

When women in the country
have to fix the fellers lunch,
it is usually cake or cookies
and it's sometimes for a bunch.

Our lunch is served with coffee
about ten or three o'clock,
unless they're driving cattle,
then you pack it in a box.

Our dinner's served at noontime
but in town it's served at night;
in the country, that's called supper.
Are you getting this all right?

If you go to town for dinner,
don't go there right at noon;
you might not get a thing to eat
because you've got there way too soon.

But if dinner's in the country
and you don't show up till eight,
you just might go home hungry
because you're half-a-day too late.

MONEY IN HORSES

"There's money in horses,"
   I once heard someone say
and I can sure attest to that,
   I worked on books today.
I kept the red pen busy
   and rarely used the black,
and please don't get me started
   on the breeding fees and tack.

The shoeing bills and vaccine
   were enough to make me choke
plus vitamins and special feed.
   It's no wonder we are broke.
Chiropractor charges
   and equine dentistry,
DNA and photographs
   plus registration fees.

It takes a lot of cash
   before a colt has hit the ground,
and even more to grow them up
   in hopes they turn out sound.
Then once that colt is broke and trained
   and good enough to show
or maybe trained for roping,
   so you can rodeo,

you'll need a truck and trailer.
   That's at least a hundred grand,
then to do the work while you are gone
   you'll need a hired hand.
So, if you want some horses,
   the best advice I'll share:
You had better win a lottery
   or just be a millionaire!

MY DRIVER

There's not much he can do now
    since he had that mini-stroke,
and the medicine they got him on
    has darned near got us broke.

Both his eyes have cataracts;
    he needs some hearing aids;
can't see or hear, but worse than that,
    his memory often fades.

He used to do a lot of work
    but now it's quite a chore
to just get up and dress himself
    and scoot across the floor.

But one thing I am thankful for,
    besides the fact he's still alive,
is when I want to go somewhere
    I still have him to drive.

NATURE'S CHURCH

Have you ever seen the prairie when it's covered up with snow,
or watched an evening sunset leave its purple afterglow?

Have you ever seen a newborn calf a-wobbling to its feet?
Although it's only minutes old it knows just where to eat.

You can't climb up in a saddle and ride across prairie sod,
or see an eagle on the wing and not believe in God.

A cowman may not worship in a building made of stone,
but worships with his Maker out with nature all alone.

His church is in the great outdoors; the valley, heaven's gate.
His favorite hymn's a coyote that is calling to its mate.

He doesn't do his tithing dropping money in a hand;
it's by being a good caretaker of the creatures and the land.

He makes his own communion while a choir of songbirds sing,
as he cups his hands to drink the fresh cold water from a spring.

From the budding of the springtime to autumn's goldenrod,
there's no better place to worship than to be out there with God.

So, when you hear a meadowlark that's singing from its perch,
it's inviting you to worship with it there at Nature's Church.

NOTHING TO DO

What do you do when there's nothing to do?
How do you know when you're done?
Do you wake every day with no plans ahead
just to wait for the setting of sun?

What do you do when you've no bills to pay
and you've got enough money to burn?
When having a job and going to work
as for you, is not a concern.

It must be real lonely with nothing to do,
'cause not many folks fit that mold.
I'd think that a friendship with someone like you
would wither and soon would grow cold.

So, don't hope for riches or fortune or fame,
and no work that's destined for you.
Be thankful for having a job everyday
or you'll end up with nothing to do.

Everything in this poem is true except for the lily pond.
This poem became my grandkids favorite bedtime story.

OAKIE and the SKUNK

Now, Pa and I were sleeping
   on that starry, moonlit night,
when Oakie started barking
   and I woke up with a fright.
I thought that I had better try
   to wake my snoring spouse
because that dog was really raising cane
   up by the chicken house.

So I woke pa from his slumber
   and I must have had him shook
because he ran right to the window,
   thought he'd better have a look.
Then his voice started trembling
   and my heart it really sunk.
when he hollered, I can see the dog,
   he's fighting with a skunk!

Then he ran across the bedroom,
   saying, I'd better get my gun,
because that skunk is chasing Oakie,
   and it's got him on the run!
Now, his guns are in a cabinet
   that is under lock and key
so it took some time to get one out
   and shells for it, you see.

Then my "Knight in Shining Armor"
   pulled his boots on at the porch
and headed out to shoot the skunk
   wearing nothing but his shorts.
I was watching from the window
   as he went into the night
in his cowboy boots and BVDs;
   it was really quite a sight!

When the skunk saw that great hunter,
    he must've sensed some harm
because he took off for an open door
    in our great big roping barn.
Well, hubby's not no dummy,
    he was not about to go
inside that big arena
    so the two could go to blows.

So, he got into his pickup truck
    and put his lights on bright
then slowly drove inside that barn,
    but that skunk was not in sight.
After shining spotlight high and low,
    the skunk could not be found
so back to bed the hunter went;
    everything had settled down.

Then Oakie started raising cane,
    and sure enough, my friends
the skunk was chasing Oakie
    as "Chapter Two" begins.
Again, I woke Pa from his slumber;
    I said, your gun you'd better get!
But the gun was in the pickup
    and that skunk was on our step!

So Pa got back in that cabinet
    and grabbed his old Twelve-Gauge;
he loaded shells and headed out.
    That skunk was in a rage!
There was fur and hair a-flying around,
    and of course, that awful stink
as I watched that brave old hunter
    from my window by the sink.

He hollered at the dog to stop;
    that skunk went running free;
with one loud blast he nailed that skunk
    right by our cedar tree.
Everything went silent
    as that skunk met his reward
but the crater blasted in my lawn
    looked like one a bomb had bored.

We scraped up what was left of it
    and put it in a sack
we took it to the local vet,
    in a day the tests came back.
He sure enough had rabies,
    so the dog was quarantined
and I fixed a nice big lily pond
    where my back lawn used to be.

But it serves as a memorial
    to that fateful, sleepless night
when I found out that our cattle dog
    could put up quite a fight;
and I also learned that Hubby,
    who I never knew could hunt,
was really quite a marksman,
    when he cratered that old skunk!

THE OLD COWBOY

I was looking around in a big shopping mall,
when out on a bench in the hallway I saw
a weathered old man in a cowboy hat;
he looked rather strange in a big place like that.

I walked up to him and I said, "I suppose
you're an old cowhand by the looks of your clothes."
"You guesses me right and a good one!" He said,
and the smell of his breath just about knocked me dead!

*"And we was lots better than these modern kids,
why, I used to run with a feller named Tibbs;
. . .can't remember his name, but at least anyways
they had tougher stock than those kids ride nowadays.*

He went on telling about years ago
when he used to win all of the big rodeos.
He rattled off names of some horses he'd rode
and according to him, he'd never been throwed.

He claimed they dogged steers that weighed half-a-ton
and roping back then had to be lots more fun,
because the calves that they roped was bigger than now;
according to him, about the size of a cow.

In a voice growin' louder, and a face turning red:
*"Who'd ever think cowboys'd wear caps on their head?
A necklace? Or earring? Why, they look a-fright!
You wear that in my day, you'd ask for a fight!*

*Their shirts look like billboards all covered with signs;
you wouldn't be caught in one back in my time!
I'll tell you right now, we were tough and were good
and we acted and dressed like a real cowboy should."*

I was beginning to wish that I never had stopped
because the longer I listened, the louder he'd talk.
I quickly changed the subject, asked where he called home;
he said: *"On a ranch, but I don't live alone*

*Because I share my quarters with my youngest grandson,
he's one of these cowboys who don't have no fun.
I call him a modern-day young buckaroo;
they never drink whiskey, don't smoke and don't chew."*

As he was a-talking, he rolled up a smoke,
then lit it and coughed 'till I thought he would croak.
That brought up something he rolled on his tongue,
then spit out what looked like a piece of his lung.

Then up walked a well-dressed and handsome young guy
who looked at the smoke as he let out a sigh,
and scolded the man for not quitting for good:
"I know that it's hard, but I sure wish you would."

He told me his name and then shook my hand,
then said: *"He's my grandpa, and quite an old man.
I sure want to thank you for listening to him;
I'm sure about the old days,"* then gave me a grin.

He helped the man up and said: *"We should go
because I have to leave for my next rodeo."*
I couldn't help notice the buckle he wore,
"NFR Champion." Must I say more?

Now folks, we've all heard it in so many ways,
how things were much better back in the old days.
I guess the old stories are like a fine wine,
they keep getting better with the passing of time.

But one thing I learned from the old man that day
was how quickly things change, and how time slips away
There's one thing for sure, we know that it's true,
... things aren't as good as what we used to do!

OLD EAGLE EYE

He can tell if a heifer is starting to calve,
    I swear from a mile away,
and see if he needs to go pull the calf
    by just simply looking that way.

He can see if a windmill is working or not
    from his horse on a faraway hill,
and tell what direction the wind's coming from
    by watching the tail on the mill.

He knows if a coyote or badger is near
    by watching the tracks in the sand,
and see if a staple is loose from a post
    on the fence that encircles his land.

He's got eyes like an eagle for finding new calves
    that their mamas have hidden all snug;
so why can't he see the mud on his boots
    that he's tracking all over my rug?

OLD FOLKS RODEO

There's a great association where old cowboys go to play,
it's like a big reunion for the hands of yesterday.
It started out "Old Timers," now they call it "Senior Pro."
They can call it what they want, but it's an "Old Folks Rodeo!"

Old Cowboys still like whiskey or a can or two of beer,
but usually bring a grandkid along to help 'em drive and hear.
They often drive big motor homes, the latest of its kind
with fancy matching trailers to pull along behind.

Their gear bags look like drugstores, full of analgesic balm,
magnets and viagra, and some pills to keep them calm.
The "chicks" that used to hang around in 1962
are now "old hens" still hanging around, and sometimes in a stew.

I thought I'd like to take one in and see how they are run
and learned that Old Folks Rodeos can be a lot of fun.
It started with the crowning of this year's Senior Queen;
I don't know the criteria, but it was quite a scene.

The one they crowned had won her banner fair and square, of course,
but when she went to run her lap she couldn't mount her horse.
Thank goodness for a gate man who helped her brace her feet,
while her predecessor pushed her rump and got her in the seat.

The entries in the barebacks are usually slim to none,
the broncs and bulls were better, though no one covered one.
They usually have some pickup men as green as they can be,
but, what-the-heck, they never work too hard, you see.

Then came the tie-down roping (that's what they call it now);
a friend of ours was entered and he caught his calf somehow.
He lumbered down and flanked that calf, one hand went underneath,
yanked that string out of his mouth, but darn! There went his teeth!

They found them when the raked the ground at barrel racing time;
those teeth were awfully dirty, caked with dirt and grime.
And speaking of the barrels, there is no where you could find
any better horses, and they clocked some real good times.

But the horses run the pattern better than their riders do,
like when 'Ol Dobbin left that gal back there at "barrel two!"
Another failed to make the turn on "barrel number one,"
but gravity has shifted since the days when they were young.

Thank God they left team roping for the last event that night;
I'll bet there were two hundred teams and it was quite a sight.
It's evident that this event is sweeping across the land,
but good old cowboys never roped with "golf gloves" on their hand.

I think old age has left some guys with not much patience left
as they sure can get upset when a partner don't connect.
One header really nailed one…might say he went for broke,
to only learn his healer had dropped his doggone rope!

I'm sure you've heard it said that every dog should have its day;
it's only right that old cowboys should have a chance to play.
So, if you crave excitement and you wonder where to go,
may I suggest you go to see an "Old Folks Rodeo."

Glen Hollenbeck on his rope horse, Fudge, who helped him win the National Senior Pro Rodeo Calf Roping (68 & over division) in 2017.

OLD NELLIE

She is sway-backed and cow-hocked,
    her jaw has got a lump;
her hair is dull and matted
    'though we worm her every month.

She's got a great big Roman nose
    and narrow, beady eyes.
She seems to hate all women
    but she nuzzles up to guys.

Her feet are big as dinner plates;
    got thighs like barrel kegs;
and you could stuff a mattress
    with the hair that's on her legs.

And every time she takes a step
    she passes lots of air,
embarrassing all the folks around,
    but she don't seem to care.

She's got an awful parrot-mouth;
    her snaggled teeth are brown;
and if she were not my sister,
    we'd have to put her down.

THE PEDIGREE

I've heard it many, many times,
    the lineage from the start
of horses living on our ranch,
    he knows them all by heart;
from Bert, to King, to Tiny Watch,
    he knows them one by one;
foundation lines of every horse,
    their daughters and their sons.

We went to lots of rodeos,
    and when we'd start for home
he'd start reciting mares and studs
    of every horse he'd owned;
and those of other ropers,
    he even knew their lines;
he knew each blasted pedigree
    until you'd think it'd blow his mind!

One time I was bored to death
    hearing which horse came from who;
I thought I'd catch him up a bit
    and throw out a name or two.
The first thing that I asked him
    was, "who was Sarah Cowles?"
I knew that really stumped him
    from the wrinkles on his brow.

He scratched his head and thought a bit,
    then said, "Now, this is strange;
I know if it's a decent line
    I would recognize the name!"
I told him he should know her;
    what I next said hurt his pride:
"It's your own grandma's maiden name
    right there on your top side!"

PERFECT GRANDPARENTS

When we raised those kids of ours,
    we did the best we could;
we tried to do things right
    so they would turn out good.
We made them use good manners
    and go to bed on time,
and lined them up with chores to do
    to earn their every dime.
They had to clean their plates up
    and learn to share their toys
and not mind wearing hand-me-downs
    from other girls and boys.
And when those kids got sassy
    or sometimes failed to mind,
they often felt some punishment
    on their little old behinds.
Spare the rod and spoil the child,
    it was a Bible rule.
The discipline our kids received
    was from the good old school!

(pause)

The grandkids came to visit us
    and spend a day or two.
We were just amazed to see
    how much that pair had grew.
They're just so smart and clever,
    and cute as they can be;
just perfect little angels,
    full of pep and so carefree.
But their mama stayed a little while
    and upset me quite a bit
when she caught them jumping on the couch
    and threw a hissy-fit.
She made them change to some old clothes
    to just go play outside

then said if they get ruined
    she just might tan their hide.
So what if they get dirty
    when they're out there having fun?
I never thought a little dirt
    should bother anyone.
She scolded them for hollering
    and making too much noise.
I told her it was quite all right,
    that "Boys will be boys."
I was glad to see her finally leave
    so they could have some fun,
and you should see the mess they made
    with grandpa's water gun.
They loved my shiny floors
    where they could run and slide.
Those black marks should come off
    with just some elbow grease and Tide.
They loved my homemade cookies
    and grandpa's candy jar,
and just like him, those Hersheys
    were their favorite candy bar.
But that mud hole in the barnyard
    was their favorite place to play
and the stock tank worked just perfect
    to wash the mud away.
But when their parents came for them,
    you should have heard them cry.
It nearly broke our hearts
    to have to tell them both goodbye.
When their parents asked if they were good,
    "Of course they were," we grinned,
then said, "We just can't wait
    to have them visit us again!"

As in nearly every family in this country, our family has had many members sacrifice for our freedom, and it is hard for me to understand why anyone would not stand and salute Old Glory, thus the reason I wrote this poem. I also appreciate the freedom we enjoy because of these sacrifices, yes, including the freedom to take a knee.

from the Revolutionary War

through the Civil War

PITY THE FOOL

They sang, "Oh, say can you see by the dawn's early light"
but you plainly can't see by your actions tonight.
When the anthem was played and folks rose to their feet,
you chose to ignore it and just stayed on your seat.

Perhaps some attention was something you needed;
if that was the case, then you certainly succeeded.
I hope you aren't thinking that you were real cool
because to most us folks, you looked like a fool.

They say, There's none so blind as those who can't see.
It seems you must be sightless as to why we all are free.
Do you think you're a hero because you're good playing ball?
The heroes folks applaud have names carved on a wall.

In fact, it would be good if you would stand before that wall
and see the names of soldiers who for YOU they gave their all;
or see a Gold Star Mother as she hugs to her chest
a flag presented to her as her son is laid to rest.

If it weren't for all those heroes, you would not be free
to sit there on the bench, or be allowed to take a knee,
It probably won't be long before your playing days are through.
Is this the way you want to have the fans remember you?

I hope you gain some sense before you play your final game,
because soon folks will forget you and will not recall your name.
'Though it seems that all bad actions are remembered, as a rule;
...your legacy will be that you were pitied as a fool.

No matter how hard we try, occasionally the efforts of a ranch wife assisting her husband are not very successful.

PULLING THE CAKING TRUCK BLUES

"The best laid plans of mice and men can sometimes go astray;"
And that is just what happened on one cold and wintery day.

I had cleaned up after breakfast and vacuumed up the floor.
I had just sat down to rest when Hubby burst into the door.

He hollered, "Come and help me! The Caking Truck won't start!"
Well, that took care of my rest as I donned my old Carhartts.

He said he had a chain hooked to another pickup truck,
and a tow might get him started with just a little luck.

Then said, "She's automatic so you best get up some speed;
I'll honk when I get started then unhook, and then go feed."

So, we got into our outfits; I got mine into gear;
gassed it good and took off when he signaled from the rear.

I heard a little noise when that log chain came up tight,
but by then I had it rolling, so I hoped things were all right.

I got it up to sixty as I headed down the lane;
the windows were fogged over, but I trusted that old chain.

It's a mile to the corner where I stopped to have a look;
all I saw was just a log chain with a bumper on the hook.

Apparently that noise I heard was the bumper coming loose,
but there's no sense speculating because my neck is in a noose.

Should I go to face the music? There's no other place to go,
so I headed back to face it, but I headed pretty slow.

With his face the shade of crimson; steam rolling from his hat;
I sensed we were not about to have a friendly chat.

Our conversation was quite short. I was quiet as a mouse.
He only said six little words, "Just Go Back to the House!"

So I heeded his instructions and with that we quickly parted.
He used some jumper cables and got his old truck started.

In a couple days he cooled down, but one thing I foresee:
The next time that he needs a tow, he sure won't call on me!

PUTTING DOWN OLD RED

It's been said that every cowboy,
   if he's lucky, in his life
has one good dog, one good horse,
   and of course, has one good wife.

To give one up is something
   we'd avoid if we could
because parting is a sorrow
   if parting is for good.

Without a doubt his best one,
   a horse he called "Old Red"
was running out of sunsets
   which is something we all dread.

But Father Time is cruel
   'though he treats us all the same;
he paid "Old Red" a visit
   and he left him old and lame.

The winters in Dakota
   can kill the young and strong
'though we kept him close and nursed him,
   we knew it wasn't long

until the weather and his lameness
   would slowly spell the end,
and no one ever wants that type of death
   for an old friend.

I felt like it was up to me,
   and something I should do,
because it's hard to put a horse down
   after all that they'd been through.

So, one day when he went riding
   and would not be home 'till night
I called a vet to help me out
   and knew it'd be all right.

After all, I wasn't so attached
　　because Red was not my mount
All the times that I had rode him
　　were just too few to count.

But by the time the vet arrived,
　　I had time to reflect
about the many rodeos
　　and money we'd collect

from all those tie-down ropings
　　that "Old Red" had helped him win,
from mounting other ropers,
　　and from picking up on him.

Then I thought about my little girl
　　when she was starting out,
how that old horse had taught her
　　what "first place" was all about.

Our trophy case is full of plaques
　　and ribbons that she won
in goats and poles and barrels;
　　my gosh that horse could run!

I went and got a halter
　　and a bucket full of oats
then dear old Red came up to me
　　and nuzzled on my coat

just like so many times before,
　　but this time was the end;
the vet was here and it was time
　　to put down our old friend.

I found out just how tough I was;
　　I guess I musta lied
when I told myself, "it won't be bad"
　　...the bad part's how I cried.

I could have filled a bucket
   with all the tears I shed,
and I hope you never face a task
   like putting down Old Red.

The Ranchwife is quite handy for opening gates, however, it sometimes takes creative persuasion to get her to go along. This poem describes one such occasion along with a description of the vehicle used.

THE RANCH RIG

He stopped by at the house to see if I'd like to take a ride,
because he was checking pastures and knows I like to help outside.

But there usually is a reason, why I'm asked to go along,
he needs someone to open gates or a calf is coming wrong.

But what causes me to hesitate and a reason to abstain
is the inside of his ranch rig, perhaps I should explain.

Have you ever seen the aftermath of cyclones or of war,
or effects from an explosion, its carnage and the horror?

Have you ever smelled a feed lot mixed with someone's garlic breath
or of decomposing mice after D-con caused their death?

Well, combine that all together and you just might have a clue
of the inside of his ranch rig that is multiplied by two.

You can't see out the windshield because of caked-on dirt and cracks;
the back one's draped with ropes and guns, twine and gunny sacks.

You could plant a garden in the dirt that's on the dash
if it weren't for gloves and papers and other types of trash.

The poor old seat has had it with springs that's poking through,
and I doubt that it's been cleaned off since the day when it was new.

You cannot even fathom the stuff that's on the floor,
and part of it falls out each time you open up the door.

There are oil cans and grease rags, a rusty can of nails,
a vaccine gun and trocar thrown inside a plastic pail.

Some used cow tags, a log chain; feed bills in there too;
pop cans, axe, and duct tape, some is used and some is new.

There's a box of fencing staples, most are used and bent,
and there's my good screw driver...I wondered where it went!

You can tell that he's been calving by the pulling chain and rag
and the odor coming from them is enough to make you gag.

I sure don't need to tell you that among this junk and crud
is hay and straw and pellets, and manure chunks and mud.

But the reason why I'm asked to go and why I hesitate
is crawling over all this junk getting out to open gates.

RANCH WIFE'S TOP TEN LIST

I don't know if Letterman had this on,
    we can't stay up that late;
but I made a list of top ten things
    that all ranch women hate.
I know I've probably missed a few
    and you could add some more,
but here's the list of top ten things
    that most ranch wives abhor.

TEN is when his minute
    turns into half a day
and plans you made were scrapped
    because of the delay.
NINE is dirty laundry
    from their socks up to their caps,
that is filthy, wet and sticky
    because of a prolapse

or perhaps they stuck a bloater
    or had to pull a calf;
and when you choke and gag,
    they look at you and laugh.
Then here comes checking pastures
    and you cannot shut a gate
because someone made it way too tight;
    that comes in Number EIGHT.

SEVEN is waiting dinner
    and trying to keep it hot
when telling you they won't be home
    is something they forgot,
because they were helping neighbors;
    it was sure an oversight;
so dried-up meat and vegetables
    is what they'll eat tonight.

SIX is backing trailers,
   those great big gooseneck kind;
and FIVE is when the truck hooked on
   has gears you cannot find.
FOUR is windy salesmen
   that always stop at noon,
and leaving they inform you
   they'll be stopping back real soon.

THREE is pulling tractors
   when it's cold and they won't start;
and why you have agreed to help
   just proves you're not real smart.
To figure out hand signals,
   that comes in Number TWO,
it's tied with pulling pickups
   that are stuck because of you.

Without a doubt, the number ONE thing
   every ranch wife hates
is when you're sorting cattle
   and her job is on the gate.
He hollers, "Hold that black one!"
   And they're all black in the pen,
and that is just the start
   of where your sorting woes begin.

As I said, there's probably lots of things
   that I have probably missed.
But there you have it, black and white,
   the Ranch wife's Top Ten List.

RANCHER WANNABE

So you want to be a rancher, well that's an easy thing to be,
    you just marry it, inherit it, or win a lottery.
It will take at least a million for a little piece of land;
    to buy a hundred cows you need at least two hundred grand.

Then you'll need to buy some bulls if you want those heifers bred
    so you'll shell out several thousand for each and every head.
A whole lot of equipment is something you will need
    for you have to put up hay and raise some cattle feed.

Of course you need good help, like a real hard-working wife,
    for you can't afford a hired man since ranching is your life.
"Good fences make good neighbors," and that saying isn't wrong
    but it costs a pretty penny if you want those fences strong.

You need corrals and working chute, a shop with every tool,
    a good warm barn, a calving shed, and gas tanks full of fuel.
You will never see the end of all the things you need to buy;
    and the fact you want to ranch makes a sane man wonder why.

It may be several years before you start to see return
    and a dollar for each thousand is the most you'll probably earn.
Your income's from the calves you raise and sell in early fall,
    but you never get to spend it because the banker gets it all.

So, unless you are a doctor that is much too over-paid,
    or perhaps a shady lawyer, then you just might have it made.
But to just become a rancher is a challenge as we know it,
    or you can pretend you are one and become a cowboy poet.

REBEL ROUSER

Perhaps it was the winter that was bad and too darned cold,
or maybe turning fifty made him afraid of getting old.
Whatever was the problem that was lodged between his ears,
the whim that overtook him nearly drove his wife to tears.

It happened one spring day last year when sorting off some cows,
and when they broke for coffee and headed to the house
he told her he was thinking that they both could use a break
and he thought a nice vacation was something they should take.

The first thing that she thought of was he'd probably want to go
to Cheyenne or to Denver to some blasted rodeo.
But he said that come next August when the haying was all done,
he'd like to go to Sturgis and take in all the fun.

He said he'd heard folks talking 'bout that rally and the hogs
and the concerts and the people; they say they come in mobs.
The first thing that she asked him was, "how the heck they'd go?"
because their 10 year-old Ford pickup would sure not fit that show.

He told her not to worry, he knew just what to do,
see, he'd seen a motorcycle that was just as good as new.
It was in the want-ad section in a paper that he'd saw
and eight hundred dollars isn't bad for a good used Yamaha.

He bought that good used cycle and he broke it in real good
as he rode around the barnyard and the whole darned neighborhood.
Then he welded up a trailer in his shop one rainy day
so they could take their tent along and have a place to stay.

She thought that he was crazy, but it got worse than that;
he started growing whiskers and let his hair grow down his back.
He said that he must look the part so he would fit right in
and told her she should get some clothes that showed a little skin.

They say she almost killed him with the look upon her face,
but it seems that it was no time when she would take her place
behind him on the Yamaha, the trailer hooked behind,
and off they went for Sturgis like the blind leading the blind.

They hadn't gone an hour on this seven-hour trip
when it felt like rigamortis had just settled in her hips.
The sun was bearing down and her skin was turning red
as thoughts of home and air conditioner were fogging up her head.

This sure was no vacation, a worse time she'd never had
and she never knew a sweaty shirt could ever smell so bad.
The blowing locks of hubby's hair was all that she could see
and anywhere besides that bike is where she'd rather be.

She begged to go back home but her voice he never heard
and he never would have stopped if it wasn't for that bird
that hit him in the face, just West of Belvidere;
it was there that he discovered her no longer in the rear.

They say a trucker found her when he stopped to check his load;
she was laying moaning...groaning in the ditch besides the road.
At first he was real startled and thought she might be dead
but the only thing that hurt her was a bump upon the head.

When hubby found she left him he at first went into shock,
. . . then he met a little dolly working in a tattoo shop.
They say he gave up ranching for his cycle and that dame
and he never works a lick . . . but it pays about the same.

The wife is with the trucker and they make a happy pair
'though she's still receiving treatment under psychiatric care.
They're trucking in the mountains for a sawmill hauling logs
and are known to mow down cycles, especially Yamahas.

So, the moral of this story is in case you need a break
and decide to go to Sturgis, please don't make the same mistake.
If you want to save your marriage, you'd better make the trip alone,
So let this be a warning gals, "Leave your husbands home!

My first published poem, unbeknownst to me, however this was what got my poetry writing out of the closet. And yes, a true event led to its writing.

ROPER'S WIFE'S LAMENT

The faucet drips and the drain won't drain
because papa has a rope horse to train.
I'm feeding the cows and milking Ol' Bess;
all papa does is the roping, I guess.

It's early to bed and early to rise...
gotta get going, gotta rope with the guys!
There's no time for dining or going to shows
because all of our spare time's for more rodeos.

There's ropes in the closet and under the chair,
you open the oven, there's one drying there.
There's ropes on the dresser and under the bed,
more ropes in the closet and out in the shed.

Him help with the lawn or the painting out doors?
He don't have the time, got to tune on his horse.
There's no extra money for shopping, you see,
for we'd just better save for the next entry fee.

For meeting my kinfolk, there's no time, of course,
but he knows all the pedigrees of every rope horse.
When I look at my daughters all I do is hope
that they marry a feller who don't like to rope!

SORTING TIME

I was hosting a Christmas Coffee,
    had my housework done up right;
I'd made the cookies and coffee,
    but my, I looked a fright.

I was standing before my bathroom mirror
    as a little fluffing up had begun
When my husband burst into the house
    hollering, "CAN YOU HELP ME HON?"

They always call you "Honey" when they need help
    don't they though?
So, I donned my boots and chore coat,
    and followed him out through the snow.

The corrals were full of bawling cows,
    their calves were bawling too,
and the only way to communicate
    was to hand-signal to the crew.

The men? They're all a-horseback,
    I'm afoot, I run the gate
where you have to be real quick to think
    and never hesitate.

You have to know when to open it
    to let out one or two,
close it quick and hook the latch
    and don't let the wrong one through!

Well, the day had started out real good
    but that soon was in the past
because tensions rise when sorting cows,
    and tempers flare real fast.

Now, back to hubby's signals ;
    I will never understand
how in this high-tech world we live in,
    there are no standard signals for the hands.

I know the one for the North corral,
    that's where we pen the bulls;
his right arm means the South corral,
    that's where we put the culls.

I turned and saw a bunch of cows
    that were headed right towards me;
both his arms were fanning the air,
    that's all that I could see.

I opened up the gate real fast,
    the cows went running out,
I closed it quick and hooked the latch;
    that's when I heard him shout:

"WHY DID YOU LET THOSE CATTLE OUT???
    GADS WOMAN DON'T YOU KNOW
I SIGNALED FOR YOU TO HEAD 'EM BACK
    AND YOU LET THE WHOLE BUNCH GO!!!"

I won't explain what next was said,
    but that ended my position,
I quit my job out helping him
    and went back to my kitchen.

But I did return one signal,
    it was directed to my loving spouse.
I'd sure lost my Christmas spirit
    when I stomped back to the house.

We had cooled down by suppertime
    and our marriage is just fine
but I'm going to cook a batch of gone
    next Spring when it's sorting time!

*A hard-working neighbor lady's comments gave
me the idea for the following poem.*

SURE A LOT OF WORK

Uncle Ralph and dear Aunt Opal
    had a pretty place, all right;
everything was painted up,
    there was not a weed in sight.

I never went to Opal's house
    when she was sitting around;
she was always out a-working
    or a grooming up the ground.

Uncle Ralph didn't work as hard
    as Opal did, you see;
like when it was time to plant the crops
    he'd only get the seed.

I don't mean to put him down
    because he was a real nice guy;
he just didn't work like Opal did,
    he just did not have much try.

One time when Opal wasn't home
    a salesman happened by;
he looked around at buildings,
    corrals and fences painted white.

Saying, "This is quite a show place!"
    Ralph gave a little smirk,
thanked him for the compliment,
    then said: "But it's sure a lot of work!"

Whenever the late Rodney Nelson or Baxter Black recited their poems about cowboy laundry, folks thought it was funny. Most women that have been on the receiving end, did not.

THE TRUTH ABOUT COWBOY LAUNDRY

Rodney and Baxter had both wrote a poem
about laundry that they had created,
But let me assure you, from the wives point of view,
their descriptions were far understated.

There should be awards such as "Tide's Purple Heart"
for the wives that are put to the test
Of handling the filthiest items on earth
and for sure the worst job in the West.

It might be a prolapse or pulling a calf,
whatever the job that gets done;
Most of the remnants ends up on their clothes
…the urine, the blood, guts and dung.

You'd lock all the doors and not let 'em come in
but none of us wives are that bold
to make them strip down outside in the yard
because the weather is usually too cold.

So here they come in; you stand there in horror
and hope that you don't have the luck
of having to help them climb out of that mess
but usually a zipper gets stuck

In their filthy old Carhartts, as your mind flashes back
to the time that you fell for this guy;
your mom tried to warn you of cowboy life
and now you can understand why.

You use a broom handle to pick up the mess
and hope that it stays on the stick;
It's a balance act that can be quite a job
because those garments are slimy and slick.

Stench fills the house and you choke and you gag
as you head for the washing machine.
You're leaving a trail that drips from the clothes,
on a floor that this morning was clean.

You dump in some Clorox, a half cup of soap
and your poor old machine goes to work;
It takes several washings before they come clean;
It's enough to make ranch wives berserk.

In the meantime you're scrubbing the mess in the house
that was tracked in or dripped on the floor,
because doing the laundry that blessed you today
is only but one minor chore.

Even the broom handle reeks of the smell
so you scrub it and spray it down good.
There's blood on the door knob, inside and out
and heaven-knows-what's on the wood.

Fresh from the shower he arrives on the scene,
says: "I'd help you if I thought I could
but the smell of that Pine Sol about makes me croak
. . . and you're just about wishing he would.

So, if your daughter is wanting to marry a cowboy
and the thought has you folks in a quandary;
the best way that I know to help change her mind
is to show her some cowboy laundry!

TRUTH IN ADVERTISING

She was lonely in the city with a life she'd learned to hate
and thought that it would help if she could find herself a mate.

For months she searched the internet, each lonely people site,
and visualized the type of man she thought that she would like.

She finally happened on one that really caught her eye
and knew at once that this would be the perfect kind of guy.

The ad read he was searching for a kind and loving wife,
one who liked to cook and would enjoy the country life.

It said he lived alone on a large Wyoming spread,
and her heart began to flutter from this post that she just read.

Romance began to spark as they courted through email,
and both were feeling certain that this match could never fail.

She caught a train to Casper; it's a good thing it was night
because vision isn't good in a railway station light.

You know how you can visualize a person and their face,
and when you finally meet them, you were really way off base?

She had seen them in the movies in all those western scenes,
and the image of a cowboy had for years been in her dreams.

Why, even cowboy poets, like the famous Baxter Black,
are tall and dark and handsome, but this dude was short and fat!

He had a big potato nose, a red and runny eye;
the cowboy that she dreamed of was a far cry from this guy.

But there's a lid for every kettle, there is soup for every pot;
for a fancy, classy city gal was something she was not.

She weighed a good 400 pounds and half her teeth were gone.
As he looked her up and down he got to thinking, "something's wrong."

But she'd come this far to meet him, so he best give her the test
to see how well she'd like it on his ranch out in the West.

The station agent told me that this pair was quite a sight
as they climbed into his pickup truck and drove into the night.

And as you might imagine, it must have been a thrill
when he told her that his home was waiting around that distant hill.

I'm sure she was surprised when he finally came to stop
before a wooden wagon with a rounded canvas top.

She asked him where his house was, and he answered "this is it!"
Although he was concerned as to how well she would fit.

Now, many days have come and gone; they make a happy pair,
although they both were fooled, but neither seems to care.

They learned a darned good lesson, and hope you have learned one too
about the ads there on the internet, to check them through and through.

Just because a man's a rancher does not mean he punches cows;
he might live on a hog ranch where he's busy pigging sows.

And every city gal may not come with savoir faire,
she might just be a "country hick" that's stuck a-living there.

So be careful of that internet; better look before you leap
or you could end up in Wyoming on a ranch a-herding sheep!

WATCH WHAT YOU PRAY FOR

I believe in God above
    and know he answers prayers.
He knows when it is dry down here
    and of course, our Savior cares.
Don't think that He's forgot us;
    He's not trying to be mean
just because it never seems to rain,
    He's testing us it seems.
Remember '97
    and all the snow we had?
We hadn't had a winter
    in a coon's age near that bad.
The feed and tanks and fences
    were all buried deep in snow
and temperatures for many days
    stayed around 15 below.

We prayed that it would warm up,
    and sure enough, it did!
That summer it got hotter
    than a boiling kettle lid.
But then we got good rainfall
    and the grass was lush and green;
the dams were running over
    as were creeks and ponds and streams.
But apparently some farmer
    couldn't plant his crops in time,
and you know when things aren't perfect,
    how they always seem to whine.
Now, please don't find me critical,
    or one to be complaining,
but I'd like to find that "so-and-so"
    that prayed that it'd quit raining!

WHAT I REALLY NEED IS A WIFE

I've got so danged much stuff to do,
I work from sun to sun;
got a great big yard to care for
and the housework's needing done.

I was cleaning out the horse barn
when I heard my hubby say
that he needed me to help him
go and mow a field of hay.

I had to run some cows in,
and fix a gate that's down
then go and get repairs
from the tractor shop in town.

There's so much work to do
when you live a rancher's life,
that I think just what I am needing
is to get myself a wife!

After spending a hot, long afternoon helping fight a prairie fire at a neighbor's place, I came home sore, tired, dirty and crabby. I turned on TV to check the weather report in hopes there was rain in the forecast, as we were in a period of drought, what I saw was Martha Stewart showing how to properly iron table linens. I have nothing against Martha, or her program (which I never watch), but it did not set well with me, and out of frustration, I wrote the following poem before I went to bed that night.

WHAT WOULD MARTHA DO?

Martha's making millions showing people how to cook
with her syndicated TV Show, her magazines and books.
But she don't know a darned bit more than gals like me and you
'though we don't get a nickel for the many things we do.

It never seems to matter when her hair gets in her eyes;
she just pulls it back and then commences making cakes and pies.
She licks the batter off her fingers right there on TV,
and why she's getting paid for it sure beats the likes of me.

I wonder if she'd fair so well if she lived on a ranch;
and what she'd use to get manure off of boots and pants.
And when she's plum exhausted and she has to feed a crew,
I sometimes stop and wonder, "What would Martha do?"

When hubby hollers that he's stuck and he could use a tow,
would she know how to find the gears and let the clutch out slow?
I wonder how she'd do sorting yearlings through a gate.
That would test her many skills . . . perhaps would be her fate.

Would she know how to fix a fence and put a splice in wire,
or use a soaked-up gunnysack to fight a prairie fire?
When she's using cream and eggs, do you think that she'd know how
to clean a hen-house, separate, or milk a kicking cow?

Her fancy TV oven, I doubt would fill the bill,
when in the house he brings a calf that's taken on a chill.
Would she know how to do the chores when hubby has the flu?
I sometimes stop and wonder: "What would Martha do?"

Last week I helped with fencing; we had to set a couple gates;
I hadn't done my housework in more than several days.
I came home sore and tired, and much to my surprise
was a couple cattle buyers, so I had to feed those guys.

And then I set another plate because guess who next arrived?
The banker, with his briefcase, came pulling in our drive.
He said that he was passing by, so thought he'd stop and look
at our cattle and our horses and he'd like to check my books.

Now folks, I'd been real busy, and my books were way behind,
but I told him he could check them, I really didn't mind,
because the records that I showed him were far from being true.
After all, I got to thinking: "What would Martha do?"

WHILE-YER-AT-IT

The first year I was "honey" until the baby came,
the twenty years that followed he used "mama" for my name.
Now he calls me "granny" and I do my level best
to not let on it bothers me and something I detest.

But the name he often uses, that's just about as bad
is "While-Yer-At-It!" That's the name that really makes me mad.
He never fails to use it when I'm headed out the door
he hollers: "While-Yer-At-It, will you help me with a chore?

Like go and feed the bottle calves and turn the water off,
'While-Yer-At-It' would you check the feed left in the trough?"
I go to town for groceries, before I get out the door,
he hollers: "While-Yer-At-It, stop by the old feed store

'Cause we need salt and mineral, then stop by at the vet
to see if Dobbin's coggins test results have come in yet."
This old "While-Yer-At-It" is disgusted through and through;
I'm about to turn the tables and call him a name or two.

But first I should advise that he had best call me "Yvonne"
or this old "while-yer-at-it" just might cook a batch of gone.
I'll tell him point blank, I'm not his granny or his mother,
…but then there is a chance I may not answer to another.

I was steaming all about this when I saw on the TV
Dr. Phil with fighting spouses when it occurred to me
that he could call me names much worse, so I best cool down
and "while I'm at it" get the stuff he needs when I'm in town.

WHOSE IDEA?

When we went to get a cow I said,
"Let's saddle up a horse."
But he told me, "No! She'll follow us right in."
After forty minutes trying,
losing patience, time and gas,
he's saddling up a horse there in the pen.

It's strange how dumb we women are
when working with our men,
and I'm sure it's not an isolated case;
but they never want the missus
to know that she is right;
I guess it's just their way of saving face.

It's a "man thing," I am certain,
but it happens now and then,
and it's something that most women will condone;
the fact that when we make
those suggestions to help out,
a good idea will soon become his own.

I asked if he would change a gate
to swing the other way,
and told him it would sure help when we sort.
Well, he was quick to tell me
that it wouldn't work at all,
and his comments were a little snide and short.

It was just a few days later
when he had to sort some pairs,
and I wasn't home to help him out that day;
when I returned I noticed
that the gate was changed around
and now it finally swings the other way.

I would probably be just as bad
if he came into the house
and made suggestions how to cook and clean,
and if he had ideas
as to how I decorate,
I'd take offense and think it downright mean.

I'll just ignore his stubbornness
and let him have his way,
for I don't care to cause a little fight;
but I'll continue sharing
my good ideas, now and then.
It's a "woman thing" to know we're always right!

One of the first things I learned when I began doing cowboy poetry at various gatherings, was that practically every cowboy poet has a poem about an encounter with a bear, thus making me believe that a bear must be a man's worst fear. I felt compelled to write one about a Woman's worst fear.

WOMAN'S WORST FEAR

We've heard a great assortment
   of encounters with a bear
and to question their validity,
   I suppose one would not dare.

Men have claimed they've wrestled them
   or roped and snubbed them tight,
and I suppose that face-to-face
   a bear could cause some fright.

Sunny Hancock gave a horse and saddle
   to a bear to ride the range;
Pat Richardson claims that Sasquatch drives his jeep,
   which I find strange.

Red Steagall sings of a bear
   that had a preacher on a limb
as the poor old parson prayed the Lord
   to not be helping him!

But perhaps the greatest battle
   between a human and a beast
was what Mable Larson had the day
   she went to get some yeast.

Now, Mable was a quiet little lady
   you may know;
a tiny little morsel
   with hair as white as snow.

She never said an unkind word,
    hardly ever got upset;
but this horrible encounter
    made her lose her etiquette.

She'd got up one spring morning,
    thought she'd bake a batch of bread,
after fixing first some breakfast
    and making up her bed.

It was right there in her kitchen
    when she opened up a drawer,
and neighbors many miles away
    heard Mabel scream in horror.

She broke a land-speed record
    as she raced across the room
screaming, "I am going to kill you!"
    As she went and fetched her broom.

She swung at everything in sight
    but missed with every swing
then grabbed the shotgun off the rack
    to kill the blasted thing!

It sounded like a war zone
    as she shot off several rounds;
those neighbors feared for Mabel's life
    from all the awful sounds.

The SWAT team soon arrived
    and found the house a total wreck,
Mabel was all right,
    but she was really on the peck

because that awful creature
    that destroyed Mabel's house
was the thing all women fear the most,
    a dirty rotten mouse!

POEMS FOR HOLIDAYS
and
SPECIAL OCCASIONS

A SENIOR NEW YEAR'S EVE

It was evening at the ranch house, the sun had just gone down;
he was thinking of the way things used to be.
It wasn't all that long ago, or that's the way it seemed,
when he was young; the West was wild and free.

That prompted him to thinking of when he was wild and free,
and my, how fast the years have seemed to roll.
The missus? She has aged a lot, her hair has turned to gray,
and the hard work that she's done has took its toll.

But what the heck, it's New Year's Eve, he'll ask her for a date;
he thinks that this will sure give her a thrill!
So he hollers: *Get your dress on, and curl up your hair!*
There's a band down at McCawley's Bar and Grill!

She answers: *What you talking about? I think you've slipped a cog!*
McCawley's closed a couple years ago!
And why the heck would we go out when you can't drive at night?
Before you ask again, the answer's NO!"

So just like every evening, he stretched out in his chair
then went looking for something on TV;
she did her Bible study, then listened to the news,
as she too thought of how things used to be.

It was darned near ten o'clock when she woke her snoring spouse,
and sent him shuffling off toward his bed;
he put his teeth to soaking in a cup there on the stand,
as she told him what the weatherman had said.

Then reminded him to take his pills and eat a couple prunes,
and hoped he'd comprehend what he'd been told;
then said, *Happy New Year honey! Some year we'll have that date;*
we'll go out and celebrate before we get old!"

ALL-AMERICAN CHRISTMAS

An All-American Christmas
   is hard to have today
with all the foreign imports
   that are packed in Santa's sleigh.
The toys all come from China,
   most clothes are from there too;
it makes me wonder if his elves
   have anything to do.

Most the trees will come from Canada,
   the trimmings from Taiwan;
as I read tags where things are from,
   I'm thinking something's wrong!
The coat I bought for hubby
   was made in Bangladesh;
his Wranglers from Korea,
   some Japanese made his vest.

And what was worse, I went to buy
   the food for Christmas Day;
the turkeys that I sorted through
   had come from Uruguay.
The hams were packed in Mexico,
   the coffee from Brazil;
that's where all the nuts came from
   except for Uncle Bill!

There's fruitcake made in Germany,
   the rum is from there too;
(perhaps that is the reason
   why poor Grandpa got the flu)
The lutefisk came from Norway,
   it smelled like something dead;
the English made the muffins,
   the Frenchmen made the bread.

Everything's from somewhere else,
 I'll tell you folks, it's sad
that an All-American Christmas
 is so hard to be had.
But from these foreign imports,
 if you'd like to find relief,
just go down to your grocery store
 and buy **American Beef!**

THE BEST GIFT I HAD IN YEARS

When you're married to a rancher and your income is from cattle,
you have to cut expenses, because saving's half the battle.

One thing we cut years ago was gifts for one another;
with kids to raise and bills to pay, there was no extra for each other.

But last year I was quite surprised when hubby said, *My dear,
the cattle markets up a bit, how about a gift this year?*

He said to drop a hint or two for what I'd like to have,
because he was heading into Winner to buy some grain for calves.

Now, Main Street there in Winner is only two blocks long,
and it don't take long to shop there, because most the stores are gone.

But, there's a jewelry store on Main Street with rings of every kind,
and I'd seen one in the window that was imprinted on my mind.

So I told him he would see it in the window of a store
on a corner there on Main Street and I hinted even more.

*It's round, and it is shiny, and I've wanted one for ages;
this one is on special and won't take a whole month's wages.*

I told him it was silver because he's a little color-blind,
and I sure don't need a big one; if it's small, I will not mind.

I knew that it'd be special as tears welled in my eyes;
I could hardly wait 'till Christmas to get my special prize!

And imagine my excitement when Christmas finally come;
no gift from him for twenty years and now he's bought me one!

Before he went to bring it in he stopped and said, *My dear,
it was more than I intended to spend on you this year.*

*but I know how bad you wanted it, you deserve the best one, hon;
they had 'em in three sizes I splurged and bought the biggest one!*

And I sure do want to thank you for describing it to me;
it was right there in the window just like you said it'd be.

Then out he went to get the gift and imagine, if you can,
how shocked I was when here he came with a real nice dog-food pan!

He went right on explaining (my jaw had hit the floor)
It was right there in the window of the local Hardware Store.

It was shiny and was silver was nice-sized and was round;
and he knew I always got upset with the dog a-eating off the ground!

He said I looked a bit surprised, and he asked me, *Why the tears?*
I told him they were happy ones, the best gift I had in years!

CHRISTMAS GRAMMAR LESSON

I know I'm not a scholar, but I'm bothered many ways
in the spelling and the grammar folks are using nowadays.

Many things we learned back in the days of long ago
have somehow changed along the way from what we used to know.

Spelling words and grammar that we used to learn in schools
apparently has disappeared with all the modern rules.

We know that Georgia starts with "George," Texas starts with "Tex",
and Christmas starts with "Christ," it don't start with an "X".

And bringing up the subject of the grammar used today,
"Merry Christmas" is the greeting that I really wish you'd say.

When you tell me "Happy Holidays", I don't know what you mean;
are you referring to July the 4th or maybe Halloween?

I hope you're not forgetting just what Christmas is about,
because your spelling and your grammar is causing me to doubt.

So this year when we celebrate the blessed Christmas day,
let's spell it right and say it right and hope folks find a way

to just say "Merry Christmas" when we honor Jesus' birth,
after all it is the top event that's happened on this earth!

DID YOU EVER THINK OF ME?

When you wrap your Christmas presents and place them by the tree
and decorate your house and yard for everyone to see;
when you plan your Christmas parties full of festive gaiety,
do you think that Jesus wonders, "Did you ever think of Me?"

There's a Santa by your chimney and reindeer on your lawn;
the lights draped on your garden fence are blinking off and on.
There're all kinds of decorations, but there's no nativity,
so, Jesus probably wonders, "Did you ever think of me?"

After all it is His birthday, but it seems that some years back
the meaning of the holiday has somehow got off track,
for the way now-days it's honored, it is pretty plain to see
how our Savior probably wonders, "Did you ever think of Me?"

You've sent a list to Santa Claus of gifts you want and need
but the greatest gift you'll ever get, you long ago received.
It came so many years ago when He died on that tree,
and He shouldn't have to wonder, "Did you ever think of Me?"

When you hear that Santa's on his way, and bringing gifts for you,
don't forget the Lord, our Savior, he may be coming too.
Although we never know just when that hour or day will be;
do you suppose he'll ask us then, "Did you ever think of Me?"

So this year when you celebrate the Christmas holiday,
take a little time for Jesus, and it wouldn't hurt to pray
and thank Him for the greatest gift that there will ever be
and He'll never have to wonder, "Did you ever think of Me?"

HALLOWEEN HEADLINES

She had been outside all day
    repairing fence the calves tore down,
when she noticed it was getting late
    and she must go to town.

The stores would soon be closing;
    there were several things they'd need
to get them through the next few days,
    like groceries, salt and feed.

The fall work's always busy
    with roundup time and weaning
so an unexpected torn-down fence
    gives "work" and extra meaning.

And when you are so busy,
    you sometimes fail to see
what day it is, or check the time,
    or where you need to be.

She'd been outside since daylight
    with no time to comb her hair
and the Carhartts that she wore for work
    received a brand-new tear.

They were stained with grease and oil
    from the tractor that she drove,
with burn holes on the sleeves
    from the branding iron stove.

She always wore those Carhartts
    when she had to help the men,
so there's bloodstains and manure
    from the cattle working pen.

But she headed into town to get supplies,
    then hurried back;
unloaded all the feed and salt
    and every grocery sack.

The next day wasn't near so bad
    until the paper came.
The first thing that she noticed
    was her picture and her name.

Right there on the front page
    of the local town's Gazette,
was the headlines and the photograph
    she never will forget.

It was of her and her straggly hair
    and dirty old Carhartts,
putting sacks into her pickup truck
    from loaded grocery carts.

The title beneath the photo
    of this awful, shocking scene,
was, "The Annual Costume Winner!"
    Yesterday was Halloween!

THE HEINOUS HUSBAND AWARD

There's a quite prestigious contest and you're about to hear
how awards are made at Christmas with one winner every year.

They list all womens' Christmas gifts, then all the gifts are scored;
the giver with the most points wins "The Heinous Husband Award!"

In this National sponsored contest, there is a real good chance
that the winner of this fine award makes his living on a ranch.

And of all the great submissions, a committee picks just two;
from the two they tap a winner; here's examples of a few.

There's Jack and Dee, the newlyweds, their first Christmas together;
they lived in North Dakota and get some awful weather.

Jack was the top vote getter back in 1992;
you see, he bought his lovely bride four-buckle overshoes.

Jane got post hole diggers from her hubby, that she loves;
and she found on Christmas morning in her stocking….elk hide gloves.

An automated vaccine gun was presented to Doreen;
her hubby won in ninety-three they thought the gift quite mean.

In ninety-four, Link won that year, his gift cost quite a lot,
and when poor Debbie opened it, they say she looked quite shocked!

She had pointed to her silverware and said that's what she needed;
he misconstrued her gentle hint, on that he soon conceded.

The gift was well-intended, but, oh my, she was torqued
when Christmas morn, the gift she got was a new four-tined pitchfork!

Last year my hubby won it, judges said he topped the lot;
he blew a lot of money because a Bobcat's what I got.

My friend had got a nice blue fox, I thought I'd like one too;
he said, "Fox don't make loaders, but the 'Bobcat' folks sure do."

So, I got this fine contraption (what I wanted was a coat);
and because this Bobcat was all mine, I had to sign the note!

But this year my step-son won it and I'll tell you folks, it's sad
because that boy looks like his mother but he acts just like his dad.

His wife had often scolded him not to litter around his chair;
she received it Christmas morning…a new trash can sitting there.

It had a bow taped on it with a note inside she read,
that he was gonna get her more but got a new shotgun instead!

So if you get a gift this year that's not to be adored,
you might submit the giver for the "Heinous Husband Award!"

HOLIDAY MAKEOVER

Let's put "thanks" back into Thanksgiving,
like we did in the not long ago
when we gathered together to thank the Lord's blessings
with family and friends we loved so.

It began with the birth of our country,
and the intentions for this holiday
was to thank the Good Lord for the bounty
of blessings that happened our way.

And let's put "Christ" back into Christmas,
and honor the birth of our King.
It's not about Santa or elves or a sleigh,
or how many presents they bring.

But a time for observing His birthday,
and to celebrate the entire Advent,
after all it's a time for observing
our World's finest and greatest event!

So, when we start out the New Year,
let's turn back the clock to the ways
when old fashioned values and customs
were the basis for these holidays.

HOW THE POOR FOLKS ARE DOING

While writing my Christmas letter,
   and was gathering up my thoughts,
I thought of all my blessings
   and folks, I counted a lot.

As I sifted through my memories,
   trying to write some Christmas Cheer;
I stopped my writing and wondered
   how the poor folks are doing this year.

I always write about the grandkids;
   we think they're pretty sweet;
they like our country way of life
   and to them it's quite a treat

To come here and help with the cooking,
   or go with the men feeding hay;
they just love it outside, but I wonder:
   how are the poor folks doing today.

Those living in some crowded city
   in a high-tech style of life;
working a job that they hate every day,
   and drowning their sorrows at night.

Of course, they make real good money,
   and out here we barely get by;
but we're rich if we count all the good things
   in our old fashioned style of life.

We all know that the cattle market
   has hit an all-time low;
while expenses have hit an all-time high
   as the politicians blow

about how good they've made the economy;
    it don't look too good out here;
but from here I stop and I wonder
    how are the poor folks doing this year.

A cold front came in yesterday
    and we got some snow last night;
those trees on the lane look so pretty
    all covered with frost, sparkling white.

There's a hawk circling over the meadow
    as the cattle graze quietly by;
a soft breeze is turning the windmill
    against a cold morning's gray prairie sky;

I feel "rich" as I gaze from my window
    and thank God for the good life out here;
from my home in Dakota I wonder:
    how are the poor folks doing this year.

O COME ALL YE FAITHFUL

They sang "O Come All Ye Faithful," but nobody came;
'guess the fellows were golfing or watching ball games
while the ladies were taking in hot Sunday sales,
or visiting salons for their hair or their nails.

The church was once full on each Sabbath day,
where families and friends would gather to pray.
And not just at Christmas, but each Sunday morn
we worshiped the day our dear Savior was born.

This was back in the day when I was a kid
and going to church was what everyone did.
Back then stores were open on Saturday night,
but on Sunday? They closed and their doors were shut tight.

But I am just as guilty like so many others,
as for going to church, I've had many druthers
like not taking the time with so much to do.
I can drum up excuses plumb out of the blue.

And then I feel bad when I learn there are scores
of churches all over that are closing their doors.
And as they are closing those doors one-by-one,
I'm sure "lack of attendance" is why they're undone.

So this year at Christmas, and throughout the year
let's help keep them open, those ones we hold dear.
Let's share Christmas glory, and remember again
the ageless old story of peace and good will to men

If it's that special meaning of Christmas you search,
don't wander away from your beloved old church
where the walls will be echoing that favorite old hymn
O Come All Ye Faithful, and "Welcome! Come in!"

There is no fiction in the following poem.

OUR FRESH CUT CHRISTMAS TREE

It seems like only yesterday when my husband said to me,
My dear, it's almost Christmastime, it is time to cut our tree.
Now, ever since this time last year I've had it in my head
that this year we'll not cut a tree but use a man-made kind instead.

I didn't know how to say just what I had there on my mind,
that the tree I wanted up this year was the artificial kind.
But out it came, and as I spoke I could tell it made him sore;
We always cut a fresh pine tree, I don't want one from a store!

Well, he was right, we always cut a real live, fresh pine tree;
we'd take the kids, the neighbors too, and it was quite a spree.
But the kids are gone, they've all grown up with families of their own
and they all have the manmade kind in their neat and tidy homes.

The neighbors? They're too busy, so I guess it's him and me
to go down to our river ranch and cut a fresh pine tree.
Well, he knew that I was busy so he said he'd go alone
and I was glad for I had lots to do so I stayed home.

It seemed like it was no time, when in the house he burst
and hollered, *Come and see our tree!* Now folks, it was the worst.
It was about the biggest tree I think I'd ever seen,
like the Christmas Vacation movie…their tree was like this thing.

I said I didn't think it'd fit through the door or in our house.
I could tell that hurt the feelings of my kind and living spouse.
He said to leave it up to him, he'd get it in all right,
so I went away and left him because I didn't want a fight.

Then a Christmas miracle happened! A friend came driving in!
He'd have help with that tree for there'd be manpower on both ends.
I can't describe the commotion getting the tree into that room;
the sounds of them shoving it through the door that ended with a boom.

They tried to stand that darned thing up but there was just one flaw,
it was way too tall so hubby said he'd go and get a saw.
He's not a real good carpenter and his tools are not the best;
the saw he brought into the house was a "chain saw," Yep. you guessed.

He trimmed it up right in the house and I know the reason why;
they got it in and to get it out they wouldn't dare to try.
Then came the big dilemma; they both were scratching heads;
just what to use for a tree stand...*I've an idea!* My husband said.

An empty metal lick tub was placed on my clean floor;
then came buckets of gravel and sand. I was standing there in horror.
They finally got that tree up and oh, my man was proud.
The finest tree we've ever had! He told his helper real loud.

Half of the room was consumed by that tree, sap on my new easy chair;
pine needles stuck in the carpet, and I was wishing that I wasn't there.
But he was so pleased with that tree, so I smiled and fought back a tear;
but let me assure you that come Christmastime, there'll be an artificial tree up this year!

THANKSGIVING ON THE RANGE

Folks living on the range
   are giving thanks most every day
   for simple things like sunshine, wind and rain.
They are thankful for a newborn calf,
   the smell of fresh-mown hay,
   or a bumper crop of newly ripened grain.

It is hard for range folks to understand
   how Thanksgiving,
   for the most part, is ignored.
How city folks have set aside
   the day for shopping sprees
   on many things that most cannot afford.

Wouldn't it be nice
   if we could just turn back the clock
   and once again to grandma's house we'd go;
to gather with our kinfolk,
   some friends and neighbors too,
   like we used to do so many years ago?

Instead of spending what should be
   a day for giving thanks
   for a campout at a local shopping mall,
to trample over others
   grabbing items off a shelf
   . . . items folks don't really need at all.

It would certainly be good
   if all the merchants closed their doors
   and the Christmas shopping frenzy was suspended;
if we gathered once again
   with our families to give thanks,
   just like this special day was first intended.

We could count our many blessings
    and be glad for what we have
    and it would surely be a welcome change
to be thankful for the simple things
    like sunshine, wind and rain,
    like a day of true thanksgiving on the range.

VALENTINE MEMORIES

It's wonderful how every year
folks send a Valentine
to ones they care a lot about
to let their love light shine.

But long ago we two agreed
that was something we'd forego;
we were building up a cow herd
and were really short on dough.

I recall back in the Seventies
when all the kids were small,
you didn't have the extra cash
to buy gifts for us all,

but you told me that you loved me
and that was good enough;
but then you sure surprised me,
let us say, you called my bluff

When you bought me those overshoes,
it was something I would need
when trudging through those sloppy pens
each time I'd help you feed.

You've always done nice things for me
to show your gratitude,
and I don't know why some folks
made those comments that were rude.

After all, back in the Eighties
when we had that awful snow,
the winds came up and temperatures
hit twenty-some below.

Those chopper mitts you gave me
sure deserved my sincere thanks;
they kept my hands from freezing
chopping ice from all the tanks.

About those plastic flowers
you bought at the Dollar Store;
they still look fresh and pretty
and who could ask for more?

But just when I was thinking
that our love light had grown cold,
the Valentine I got this year
was like the mother lode.

It is just what I'll be needing
when we get some warmer weather;
some brand new post hole diggers
so we can go fix fence together!